Finding the GOD ZONE

Finding the GOD ZONE

Where Hope Lives

TANA ALCORN

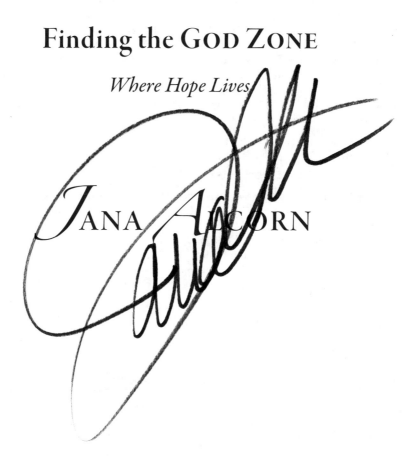

DESTINY IMAGE® PUBLISHERS, INC.

P.O. Box 310, Shippensburg, PA 17257-0310

"Speaking to the Purposes of God for This Generation and for the Generations to Come."

This book and all other Destiny Image, Revival Press, MercyPlace, Fresh Bread, Destiny Image Fiction, and Treasure House books are available at Christian bookstores and distributors worldwide.

For a U.S. bookstore nearest you, call 1-800-722-6774.
For more information on foreign distributors, call 717-532-3040.
Reach us on the Internet: www.destinyimage.com.

Trade Paper ISBN 13: 978-0-7684-3218-3
Hardcover ISBN 13: 978-0-7684-3395-1
Large Print ISBN 13: 978-0-7684-3396-8
Ebook ISBN 13: 978-0-7684-9075-6

Previously Published as:
Don't Throw in the Towel: Hope Again!
ISBN 978-0-9798380-0-2 © 2007
Study Guide ISBN 978-0-9798380-1-9 © 2009

For Worldwide Distribution, Printed in the U.S.A.
1 2 3 4 5 6 7 8 9 10 / 15 14 13 12 11 10

Dedication

To Jordan, my amazing son:

We have walked together through some of the most devastating places in life. You have shown such courage and trust in the Lord when our hearts and lives were so broken. Our family will be together again in Heaven someday. I love you!

—Mom

Acknowledgments

Special thanks to Don Nori Sr., Don Milam, and all the Destiny Image team. You publish hope.

Honor to my bishops and pastors—I am grateful for your love and wisdom through the most painful season of my life. You live hope.

Endorsements

I have had the privilege of knowing Jana Alcorn for the past decade or so. She is a remarkable woman of God with a powerful anointing to ground and guide the people of God into the fullness of His purposes in their lives. Her journey has not always been an easy one; clearly, she tasted multiple tragic events over the course of about five years, causing her to feel the weight of heaviness press deep into her soul and spirit. Yet this amazing woman found God in a new way as she learned how to process her pain, turn her pain into promise, and then turn promise into life-changing power. Her newest release, *Finding the God Zone*, will provide you a clear pathway to experience genuine hope—no matter how much pain or despair you have encountered.

If ever there was need for a word on hope, it is now. And, if ever anyone had the "right" to speak on how powerful hope is, how it brings us into "finding the God zone," and how it becomes the foundation for mountain-moving faith, it is Jana. She has that word on hope, and it's in this powerful volume you are about to read. Take your time as you read of Jana's own journey. Then let her lead you through the texts in the Word that will speak to the rough terrain in your own heart and spirit that need to be made smooth and whole. This is a life message. It will bring genuine hope from the God of hope and will fill you with a newfound appreciation for His presence in your life.

Thanks Jana, for being so transparent about your personal journey. It is a healing balm to all of us.

Dr. Mark J. Chironna
The Master's Touch International Church
Mark Chironna Ministries

I have known Jana Alcorn for over two decades and can say that she is one of the most inspiring and encouraging writers, speakers, humanitarians, and leaders that I have ever come in contact with. She has taken every hardship of life and translated it into a message of hope that resonates with life to everyone she comes in contact with. Her story is one of tragedy and triumph; but the most amazing thing about Jana Alcorn is that, even though she has come through the fire, you never hear the sound of despair in her voice or smell the scent of smoke upon her garments of praise. I recommend her writings and her ministry to anyone and everyone. Few people have captured the message of hope and grace more than Jana Alcorn. She could have been somewhere in a fetal position singing the blues, but instead she is taking hope and restoration to the ends of the earth. When you encounter Jana Alcorn, you encounter abundant life and discover what hope restored can do for you. My highest recommendation goes to this woman of God, my friend, Jana Alcorn.

David R. Huskins Th.D., D.D.
Presiding Archbishop
International Communion of Charismatic Churches
Cedartown, Georgia, and Buffalo, New York

Table of Contents

Introduction

How would you like to wake up every day with fresh anticipation of walking in the hopes of the Lord for your life? How would you like to face every circumstance deeply understanding the true Source of hope? How would your life be different if your mind-set were riveted to that hope on a daily basis?

What I am about to share with you is going to change your life. I know what it is to face day after hopeless day. Yet, I also know the joy of exiting the basement of life and seeing the sunshine again. Whatever it is that you are going through, or whatever it is that you have come through, God is right there with you, *now!* You can hope again, no matter what has happened in your life. You can live with a sense of awe in His amazing expectation for your journey.

I write this from the other side of an avalanche. One horrendous thing after another struck my life. Several life-altering events happened all at once and piled up over me. I dealt with a lot of loss in a short period of time. I was forged in the place of pain; however, I discovered that our lives are not entirely about the pain, disappointment, loss, and hurt. Our lives are about the glorious hope and purpose that God has planned for us, even before we were born. The good news is that God never consults our past to determine our future.

> *I wait for the Lord, I expectantly wait, and in His word do I hope* (Psalm 130:5 AMP).

Hope Can Be Restored!

The Bible teaches that *"Hope deferred maketh the heart sick...."* (Prov. 13:12).

We can learn much from this verse. If delayed hopes and unrelenting disappointments have the capacity to leave you heartsick, then the inverse is also true: When hope is given, the heart is made whole. Then, vision can be restored, and it becomes clear again that God has a plan for your life.

Is your faith being tried by fire? It is not over! I stand in agreement with you for the restoration of hope and the recovery of purpose in your life. Your "hope destiny" is calling. He is the God of the *now*. Your ability to hope might have been damaged—maybe it is dead and needs to be resurrected. You might not feel hope; you might not even have the faith for it. Yet God is with you in your today. Therefore, your hope in Him is positioned to incubate and grow stronger.

Get ready for hope to give birth to faith for your life—beginning *now*.

CHAPTER ONE

There Really Is a God Zone!

What do you do when the worst possible thing happens? In the span of four years, I helped plan five funerals. All of them were for members of my immediate family. The first funeral was for our daughter; the fifth was for my beloved husband.

You can imagine that I was shaken to my core. In the midst of all the tragedy and heartbreak, everyday life continued: daily challenges, personal wilderness journeys, and several once-in-a-lifetime transitions converged in one incredibly intense period of time. It was more than I could bear.

Monumental pain is something I know firsthand. From 2001 through 2005, I experienced the most relentlessly purging years of my life. Our 20-year-old daughter, Hayley, who was my stepdaughter, was killed in a tragic car accident in 2001, just weeks after the horrific terrorist attacks of September 11. Six months later, we buried my mother-in-law. One month after that, we said goodbye to one of my best friends ever, my dad. The following year, my father-in-law died of bone cancer.

Then just months later, my husband died in my arms as our 12-year-old son, Jordan, sat with us at his dad's bedside. As I contended with loss and its implications, I found myself hacking through a wilderness of my own, stopping to bury my loved ones while navigating through the harsh terrain of life's stunning experiences.

Beyond human consolation, the depths of my despair incarcerated my soul. Characterized by a tangible darkness, the seconds of each hopeless day seemed to drag on for eternity. Motherhood, the one remaining cherished aspect of my life, now mocked me as I looked at our son and wondered how I could possibly raise him amid the emotional devastation permeating our lives.

With most of Jordan's immediate support system gone, I knew my son deserved the full attention of his remaining parent. He was worthy of a mom who could be totally and joyfully present to each of his days. Yet, how was I to find the wherewithal to be that kind of mother?

Panic, fear, and helplessness engulfed me. Not only did they surround me, they spoke to me. Like built-in software voice prompts, they said:

"You are not fit to be a mother to your son."

"You are never coming out of this."

"Your life is over."

"You can't make it on your own. The pain will never stop. You might as well end it all now."

As I opened each new day, the voices spoke. On and on, over and over again, the software of my being was infected with a virus called *hopelessness*. With each beat of my heart, the virus spread throughout my life.

Without the man who vowed to love and treasure me forever, and without the cherished family life that we knew, I was left standing, languishing, in the middle of ruins. When I inventoried the aftermath of devastation, I didn't see how I could ever live, much less thrive, in the face of so much loss. My train of life had been derailed, and I was injured; in fact, emotionally speaking, I was bleeding to death.

About a week after my husband's funeral, our son went back to school. One of Bill's daily joys was to drive Jordan to the middle school he attended. The first few morning drives to school without him racked us with the pain of overwhelming loss. I tried to make things as comfortable as I could for our grieving son, but I know I didn't do a very good job. Not wanting him to see me totally wrecked, I put on my daily driving-my-son-to-school face. Then, instead of going back home, I would drive for hours and hours until it was time to pick him up again, wearing my everything-is-all-right face. No one but God truly saw me in this broken down, hurt, battered, damaged condition.

One morning, after dropping Jordan off at school, I reached a severe breaking point. Instead of taking my usual drive, I went back to our house. My mom, who had moved in to help me with Jordan, was standing at the kitchen sink, about to load the dishwasher. When I walked through the door, I saw her standing there, dish towel in hand.

Normally, anytime I came into the house, I went straight to the back bedroom so that I could immediately hide the pain. On this day, however, I stumbled into the kitchen, slammed the door behind me, turned to the laundry room door and began to beat the door, screaming, crying, yelling in excruciating bursts of pain, "Bill! Bill! Bill! Bill! Bill!"

Exhausted, I fell to the kitchen floor, screaming in agony, hitting the floor until my hands and fists could take no more. Bill was not coming back, and I was losing it.

I picked myself up and ran out to the car, ignoring my mom's call. I planned to take another drive in which there would be another screaming and crying session; but this time, I knew it was the end.

"I can't take the pain anymore. If You are through, I am through," I screamed at God, with tears splashing down my cheeks.

As far as I was concerned, I could not go on. I couldn't raise our boy like this. How was I supposed to bring healing to his aching heart with my own heart ripped out? Jordan deserved better than what I could give.

The only meaning of life left for me was to raise our son, but my ability to do so had been stripped away by one disastrous storm after another. I only knew one way out.

That was when I ran to what I call the *God Zone.*

Is your faith being tried by fire right now? Are you where I was with your emotions teetering on the brink of collapse? Has your hope taken an overdose of sleeping pills? Do not give up! He is the God of *all* hope. Go to this unmovable God Zone and trust in Him. Let Him take you where your natural mind or circumstances are powerless to go.

God: Real? Exists? Loves Me?

This is the place in every man and woman that cries out for a Being who is greater than our circumstances, greater than our intellect, greater than our abilities to network, greater than our schemes and dreams.

Within each of us lies the desire to connect with our Creator in a very personal way.

Dr. Carl A. Hammerschlag, a doctor who has followed much of the research on prayer studies, stated:

> Connecting to something other than self, something that inspires you, something that fills you with awe and love; they all embolden the healing spirit.[1]

This is the place I call the God Zone. It is the place where we acknowledge that He is real, that He exists, and, yes, that He loves us infinitely and completely.

It is in this womb of hope in Him that we can give birth to anticipation and expectancy. It is here that we can believe that He holds the future, even when we do not know what the future holds. It reminds me of childhood; I can recall my simplistic approach to knowing that God was in control of our lives and understanding that His control included everything that He would allow me to experience.

From my half-pint vantage point, all I could see was the tall grass. I heard my parents call it *Johnson grass*. I never knew the mysterious Mr. Johnson who had the tall grass named after him. Yet, I did know that if I sat down in the middle of it, the stuff would be way over my eight-year-old head.

With my school-distributed Gideon Bible in my hand, this Johnson grass provided the secret place I needed, to shut myself in with the Lord. This would be among my first encounters in the God Zone. It was here in the cotton fields of Alabama where I had my initial confirmation that, *yes*, God does exist. *Yes*, He is real, and *yes*, He does love me.

This serene, pastoral atmosphere in the field with amber waves of grass dancing over my head would too quickly give way to the often cruel vicissitudes of life. At this tender age, I could never have imagined the many opportunities life would present to challenge my belief in the God Zone.

Not that the Bible lacks examples of such challenges. There are more than enough examples in the Word of God to teach us about life's difficulties. Job might be the quintessential example. This Old Testament man's trials made him a legend.

But his fame came with a price. He felt himself devoid of God's tangible Presence for many days—so much so that he said, *"My life drags by—day after hopeless day"* (Job 7:6 TLB). Yet, despite his season of spiritual drought, Job understood and knew that there was a God Zone, a place of a higher existence.

Job experienced the gamut of emotions. He had serious moments of depression. There were days when he felt forsaken by friends and family, even abandoned by God.

My kinsfolk have failed, and my familiar friends have forgotten me. They that dwell in mine house, and my maids, count me for a stranger: I am an alien in their sight (Job 19:14-15).

My breath is strange to my wife, though I intreated for the children's sake of mine own body (Job 19:17).

All my inward friends abhorred me: and they whom I loved are turned against me (Job 19:19).

Have pity upon me, have pity upon me, O ye my friends; for the hand of God hath touched me (Job 19:21).

But because Job had a core belief in the God Zone, he was able to say, in spite of the feelings of depression, loneliness, betrayal, rejection, etc.:

I know that my Redeemer lives... (Job 19:25 NKJV).

Job believed in the God Zone. As a small child, learning to take care of the animals, I am sure that Job would never have dreamed of the challenges that would come into his life and test his core belief in a merciful God.

I grew up in the cotton fields of Alabama. Life was always supposed to be simple there. As a child, the greatest challenge I faced was wondering whether Momma would let me ride on the back of her cotton sack until she got to the end of the cotton row.

My mother often got us up early in the morning to ride in the back of a rickety pickup truck as we headed for Paw Paw's cotton farm. I have vivid memories of jumping up and down on top of the freshly picked cotton. Life was wonderfully simple.

However, the trials of life come suddenly. They challenge our faith and our hope. Persistent voices tell us that we might as well give up, because God is not going to move on our behalf. These voices even tempt us by asking, "Suppose there is no God? Then what will you do?" These voices can only be quenched by the shield of faith that God provides for every believer.

First, however, you must establish your God Zone. You must settle the fact that He does exist; He is real; and He does love you. You must come to the understanding that His love includes a relentless passion to put you in the place of your destiny and give you a future and a hope.

For I know the thoughts that I think toward you, saith the Lord, thoughts of peace, and not of evil, to give you an expected end (Jeremiah 29:11).

This core belief in the God Zone will be your very first breeding ground for hope. Each of us has been invited to come boldly before God's throne of grace. But to take that step, we must first believe that God really does exist.

…he that cometh to God, must believe that He is, and that He is a rewarder of them that diligently seek Him (Hebrews 11:6).

This is our call to prayer. It is our invitation to come and tell our

King all that is in our hearts. It is an open, come-as-you-are summons. This invitation to come to God cannot be viewed as one of many routes to hope. No. We must have an understanding that there is *no* hope apart from God, and Jesus is the only door to the real hope God offers.

In order for hope to be nurtured, you must—and I mean *absolutely must*—develop your prayer life. Hope is always nurtured by prayer. I first learned this important lesson as a child when an accident forced me to the place of prayer.

"Somebody help me, now!" I screamed. My cousin's seemingly life-less body was now curled up inside my arms. The skateboard was a new trend back then. By the time my cousin and I had reached the end of the sidewalk, we had both tumbled onto the concrete, her head splitting wide open. My cousin was only four years old. As her crimson blood gushed down onto her shirt, her grandpa heard my cry for help. He ran up the country road to her aid and rushed her to the hospital.

There was no time for anything but prayer. Yet, the ride to the hospital was the longest ride of my preteen life. Would my cousin live? Would her beautiful face be scarred for life? I wondered many things but could only pray one word: *Jesus...Jesus...Jesus...Jesus!* All the way down the road, I spoke His name.

Prayer is powerful, even from the lips of a child. My one-word prayer was born from a heart of simple trust. It was in this uncomplicated place of prayer that hope was first nurtured in my life. It proves that, no matter how small your step of hope might be, it is still a step. Our heavenly Father loves even our baby steps.

Prayer Is the Breeding Ground of Hope

One of my favorite names of God in the New Testament is "the God of all hope." I just love that! The great apostle Paul used it in his epistle to the believers in Rome. His prayer for them was powerful:

Now the God of hope fill you with all joy and peace in believing, that ye may abound in hope, through the power of the Holy Ghost (Romans 15:13).

Simply stated, Paul told them that even while praying, that they would be abounding in hope. Prayer is the nurturing place for hope; hope is the womb of faith; and faith in God can turn your situation around. Hope can break the bondage of discouragement. Go to God often in prayer to reinforce in your heart the power of His Word and the power of His Presence. You will see that hope will be incubated in this place of prayer.

Your place of prayer might be small, but it is the most significant place in your life. It is where you are going to begin to foster hope. As a result, hope is going to live again in your life—and not only live, but thrive and flourish and grow and multiply.

In the Old Testament, when Esther faced the annihilation of her people and there seemed to be no hope, she ran to the place of prayer. She could have turned to tactics of the flesh and utilized her natural skills. She could have used her beauty, but instead she went to God.

*Go, gather together all the Jews that are present in Shushan, and **fast** ye for me, and neither eat nor drink three days, night or day:*

*I also and my maidens will **fast** likewise; and so will I go in unto the king, which is not according to the law: and if I perish, I perish* (Esther 4:16).

Prayer is the conception chamber of hope for your tomorrows, and it will breed faith for your todays. The reason it is so important to build your hope is this: The hope you have today for tomorrow will become faith when tomorrow gets here. Hope is future-minded. Faith is for now. If you don't have hope for tomorrow, you'll never have faith when you get there. We must have faith for each new day.

Since prayer is so important, we need to know what it is. Prayer is talking to the Lord as you would talk to your best friend. I've discovered that doing menial household tasks can provide golden opportunities to pour out your heart to the Lord. Years ago, He had given me a simple, yet intimate, meaning of prayer.

The morning had begun as usual with hot coffee and a bacon-and-eggs breakfast. I was going to clean up quickly and start a very ordinary day. As I finished washing the last dish, my heart began yearning for the Presence of the Lord. The kitchen sink had become my altar of prayer. With my arms soaked up to my elbows, I heard Him speak so plainly, almost audibly. I didn't know it, but I was about to hear one of the most profound definitions of prayer; it came as the Holy Spirit lingered in my kitchen. He whispered to my soul and described prayer as *"the gushing of the heart toward God."*

He knows the inarticulate groans that come from the deepest reservoirs of our hearts. Prayer is a matter of the heart, and He longs to meet us there.

You Are Never Alone!

"I don't mind dying for dying's sake, but I don't want to leave you and Jordan," Bill painfully shared. With these words, I pressed my tired face and weeping eyes against Bill's warm, broad chest. Only days before, we had gotten a phone call that would forever alter all of our lives.

From the moment I laid eyes on him, Bill's heart of tenderness for others was compelling. That same tenderness was poured into my life time after time after time in almost 20 years of marriage. Bill had always been my best friend, my pillow, and my pillar. His own struggles and trials had tempered his life with an understanding that is rare. At a little over 6 feet tall, his presence was larger than life. So were his signature teddybear hugs and his compelling gentleness.

Together, we had weathered severe storms and tragic losses, including the deaths of our daughter, his Mom and Dad, and my Dad. Even when we faced the deepest pains of life, at the end of the day, we always had each other. Now we were facing another crossroads and were unprepared for the decisions that we would have to make. Even then, at least we had the comfort of each other.

All of that was about to change. I had, tucked away in my heart, a special verse and now it came to mind: *"What time I am afraid, I will trust in Thee"* (Ps. 56:3). God knew I was certainly afraid.

I wasn't sure if I totally knew what an oncologist was; I wasn't even sure I could spell it correctly. When you have to walk these things out in your own shoes, they take on a whole new significance. Both Bill and I had spent years in college, but neither of us had ever before sensed the vivid reality of the word *oncologist*.

All of a sudden, the "what-ifs" of this dreaded disease and prognosis filled my mind. Would he die quickly? Would his body deteriorate before our eyes? Would he go into a coma? Would the chemotherapy make him sick? What about the financial pressures on our family? What about the psychological effect on our 12-year-old son?

Fear and panic began to invade. I tried to turn my back on it and walk away, but my silent tears were unstoppable. "Has our family not been through enough? Why did God have to let this happen? Is God really with me? Is He here? I feel so all alone."

On August 11, 2005, at 7 o'clock in the evening, Heaven made an extraordinary visit to Room 302 of a hospital that was very special to us. Bill had been admitted to the hospital just 20 hours earlier. With each passing agonizing moment, his breathing was more labored, and he spoke very little. Sitting beside the bed, I heard him mumble a question. "What are they saying?" he muttered with closed eyes. I squeezed his hand and assured him gently. Immediately, he said to me, "Oh! It's glorious!"—as if he had been ushered into an arena of angelic bliss and heavenly activity beyond description! I had never heard Bill use the word "glorious" in all of our years together. My heart leaped as I moved from the bedside chair to his bed, the tears silently falling from my eyes. This could be his invitation to another world, I thought, a heavenly world where cancer or pain can never enter! Sitting there, I felt the Presence of the Lord and knew that the door of Heaven had been opened. I said through my anxiety and pain, "Yes! It is! GO!" Within seconds, our family and friends had been called to the bedside of my husband as he transitioned from this life to the next. Strange how life can be a series of the deepest joys and the deepest pains. It was this same hospital that Bill and I had walked out of on a hot July afternoon, carrying our 7-pound, 8-ounce bundle of "Jordan angel" in our arms. That was just 12 years earlier. Now, as Jordan and I were making our way back to the car, one of us was missing: Dad was now with Jesus.

I pulled our son into my arms. "Son, there was a day that Dad and I walked into this hospital as two people, and came out three. Now, we have walked in here as three people and come out two." God was going to have to help us make it through this agony that hurt so bad. We ached.

Bill's home-going service was a precious celebration of his life and also gave honors to his military service in the U.S. Air Force. Ultimately, his patriotic passion was responsible for the ingestion of the deadly Agent Orange that brought on the fatal lung cancer.

That afternoon, our home was full of committed friends and family. In spite of the loving compassion that surrounded our son and me, my heart was in shards. I did not know of a single way to express this to anyone. The accumulated pain of the past few years had gone too deep. Now, the loneliness and emptiness tried to mutter loudly—*Mayday! Mayday! Life Is Crashing Uncontrollably!* The thoughts were there, but their expression could not be articulated.

In the days ahead, the silence of our lives would be deafening.

"Mom, I would take Dad back right now, even with cancer," Jordan said as he pointed to the empty place where Bill's hospital bed had been only hours before. I had prayed over our son as he said goodbye to five immediate family members: sister, grandmother, grandfather, another grandfather, and now his dad. We ached. We were lonely. So lonely. This was not just ordinary loneliness; it was over-our-heads loneliness.

Dark shadows of grief engulfed us, but we were never alone. Jesus had said that He would never leave us nor forsake us (see Heb. 13:5) and would be with us through every season of life. I knew that He said it, but it just didn't *feel* like it.

As I glanced from the master bedroom to the bath, I noticed Bill's electric razor on the countertop. As he did daily, he had just shaved yesterday. Now, he was gone. Looking farther to the right, I saw his favorite toothbrush. Boy, he sure needed a new one! Well, he would have needed a new one. Similar scenarios would be repeated time after time in the coming days. All of this would be further evidence that Bill was not coming back. My hope tank had never been so depleted.

Unreservedly, day after day, I would pour my aching soul out to the Lord. Maybe there are times when your prayer is really nothing more than lashing out at the Lord. He understands. Just keep letting Him know how you feel. Jesus is our High Priest, and He lives to make intercession for each of us (see Heb. 3:1; 7:25).

You are never alone in this place of prayer, for there is always One interceding for you and with you.

> *Therefore He is able also to save to the uttermost (completely, perfectly, finally, and for all time and eternity) those who come to God through Him, since He is always living to make petition to God and intercede with Him and intervene for them* (Hebrews 7:25 AMP).

God knows your place of brokenness. He is so passionate about His people, and the Holy Spirit is sympathetically brooding over the intercessions of our Chief Intercessor, Jesus Christ. Through your hurt, you might be able to do no more than moan a few indistinguishable mutterings. That is OK. The Holy Spirit is well able to take those before God's throne of grace.

This is the work of the Holy Spirit pleading and interceding through us, even when we do not know that He is doing so. One of the meanings of intercession is "to come between."[2] We do not know the things that our intercessions *are* holding back. The Holy Spirit comes and offers Divine intervention when we pray and yield to Him in prayer.

Intercession also means "to strike upon, to assail one with petitions, to come between, to urge."[3] Intercession is one of the highest forms of prayer; it allows you to become aggressive, get on the offensive and move God's plan from Heaven to earth. This is the time to fight for deliverance. He is still on the throne.

With Bill in Heaven, I was left alone to try to explain life to our young son. At bedtime, Jordan said, "Mom, Dad didn't get to fulfill His purpose in life because his purpose was to raise me, and I'm not raised." He muttered agonizingly, his eyes filling and running over with tears.

It had been only hours since the funeral service had ended and our guests and friends started leaving our home. It was the hour of the night when Bill and Jordan would always follow up their evening snacks with bedtime prayer. Now, kneeling down beside Jordan's bed as I had seen Bill do every single night, a shadow of heavy grief was cast over our lives. How would I answer such an honest question from the heart of a wounded son?

"God, You have to help me, now. Please give me words to say."

My heart appealed for God's help as I proceeded to answer Jordan's question. "Son, we don't always understand why things happen the way they do in this life. But for some reason, Dad's purpose is in Heaven now, while ours is still on the earth," I sighed with pain.

I knew I didn't have all the answers, but I knew that the Holy Spirit was present. I felt as though a volcano of emotional pain was about to erupt. Yet, I knew by faith that He was there. I didn't *feel* Him, but I understood that He would never leave us.

God understands the cry of your heart. The Spirit interprets these cries of pain, desperation, and anguish. This is what happened to the children of Israel. God heard their heart's cry when they were oppressed.

During that long period, the king of Egypt died. The Israelites groaned in their slavery and cried out, and their cry for help because of their slavery went up to God (Exodus 2:23 NIV).

The children of Israel cried. There is a cry that God cannot deny. The price of this kind of cry is often isolation and, at times, the most excruciating inward pain. This level of crying is usually born out of life's most painful calamities. That is the time for you to see the love of God in action.

It is the passion of God's heart for His body to function in full compliance with His original plans and purposes. This cry is a human lament with no natural remedy. It is a kind of anguish or burden that comes from within and produces a sighing, a cry of the compassionate heart of even God Himself on your behalf.

Let your own human cry go out to God. It's about giving up your control of every situation and depending solely on the Master. His pleading heart yearns for you to see His hand. When this happens, it will not be long before manifestation. God does not forget our cries, and there is a cry that God cannot refuse. Birth pangs always come before birth. Sound always precedes manifestation. The hope that you desire is about to manifest.

> *The first thing I want you to do is pray. Pray every way you know how, for everyone you know* (1 Timothy 2:1 MSG).

> *I know, Lord, that our lives are not our own. We are not able to plan our own course* (Jeremiah 10:23 NLT).

> *Let the priests, the ministers of the Lord, weep between the porch and the altar; and let them say, Have pity and spare Your people, O Lord, and give not Your heritage to reproach, that the* [heathen] *nations should rule over them or use a byword against them. Why should they say among the peoples, Where is their God?* (Joel 2:17 AMP)

> *All the time that Peter was under heavy guard in the jailhouse, the church prayed for him most strenuously* (Acts 12:5 MSG).

> *And I will pour upon the house of David, and upon the inhabitants of Jerusalem, the spirit of grace and of supplications...* (Zechariah 12:10).

> *Likewise the Spirit also helpeth our infirmities: for we know not what we should pray for as we ought: but the Spirit itself*

_____

_____

_____

_____

_____

_____

_____

_____

_____

_____

_____

_____

_____

_____

_____

_____

_____

_____

_____

_____

_____

_____

_____

_____

_____

Hope
Journal

Hope
Journal

CHAPTER TWO

This Is Working for You

Consider Abraham in the Old Testament. He had amazing promises from God, yet he went through trying circumstances. No one on this earth has a problem-free life. In fact, life sometimes writes you a check and expects you to go out and cover it. Even so, this is working for you.

> *For our light affliction, which is but for a moment, worketh for us a far more exceeding and eternal weight of glory...* (2 Corinthians 4:17).

> *We know that all things work together for good to them that love God, to them who are the called according to His purpose* (Romans 8:28).

Does it ever seem that you have died and been laid in a stony grave with the boulders of life rolled in front of the exit and your resurrection permanently delayed?

God never wastes the in-between times. The time between the crucifixion and the resurrection is valuable to the realm of the Spirit of God, as well as your spirit. In the midst of what you think is the end, you will find what is really the beginning. Jesus did not come only to die; He also came to rise from the dead. It was in rising from the dead that our salvation was obtained.

If Christ be not risen…your faith is also in vain (1 Corinthians 15:14).

This is the time for a fresh demonstration of faith, spawned by a new revelation of hope. It was only after His passion, after His suffering, that He showed Himself alive. God is getting ready to show that you are really alive—that you are not dead and the battle did not kill you, but actually drove you to the place of consecration and surrender as never before. Everything that has happened can be a vehicle to move you closer to His purposes for your life.

Your Wilderness Is a Passageway

The famine that you have faced, the wilderness that you thought would kill you is, in fact, one of the passageways that God used to position you for your promised land. God's divine intention for you is so great. Do not insult the intelligence of God by judging yourself on the basis of where you are now. The cross seemed so opposed to God's intentions—until after the resurrection!

If you have been through a "crucifixion experience," don't stop now! You must learn to deal with high-level demonic forces that come against your mind in order to achieve God's destiny for your life. Even when all the evidence is contrary, God's ultimate plan of hope is still on.

God Has Factored in All Things

Prepare for what God has in His mind, not what you have in your mind. Please inform all of your enemies that you are tailor-made for God's assignment and that He has already factored in every trial, battle, hindrance, report, weakness, failure, circumstance, rejection, abandonment, and every obstacle in the Christian race. You need to declare to every obstacle: *Don't even try to hinder me now because God has written my name on His agenda, signed it in the blood of Jesus, and no weapon formed (and I mean no weapon), whatever it may be (and I mean whatever), can possibly prosper!*

> *But no weapon that is formed against you shall prosper, and every tongue that shall rise against you in judgment you shall show to be in the wrong. This [peace, righteousness, security, triumph over opposition] is the heritage of the servants of the Lord [those in whom the ideal Servant of the Lord is reproduced]; this is the righteousness or the vindication which they obtain from Me [this is that which I impart to them as their justification], says the Lord* (Isaiah 54:17 AMP).

You Are Tailor-Made for This

You are tailor-made for this, even for the battle. There are some things that you are made for, and this is one of them. Whatever your design, your makeup, your uniqueness, God has made you for your assignment.

Do you understand the stripping process that you have been through? Start asking yourself the right questions: "Am I here because of sin and rebellion? Am I here because of a lack of knowledge? Am I here because God alone knows that, from this position, I can get to where He wants to take me for His glory? Or am I here because I am not exempt from the human race and life happens to all of us?"

In the wreckage of crushed dreams and broken lives, I am convinced that we humans are not going to understand why some things happen in our lives. We never get to choose the entire script of our lives. Remember, through all the most difficult seasons of life, He is writing your story with a heart of love and purpose. I can tell you that God will not waste one thing that happens to us. He will use all of our circumstances to help others to experience Him as the God of all hope. We cannot change our past. We cannot change what happened five minutes ago. But what we can do is allow Him to take the pain and the darkness and the loneliness and draw us close to Him so we can be a light of hope to others in despair. We are called to simple trust.

Life happens.

"I have never had clarity," Mother Teresa is quoted as saying, "What I have always had is trust."[1] Trusting God isn't always easy.

Though the mountains be shaken and the hills be removed, yet My unfailing love for you will not be shaken nor My covenant of peace be removed (Isaiah 54:10 NIV).

A Great Vision **and** a Great Person

You might have a great vision, but God wants to make you a great person. God loves you and has a plan for your life! Persevere!

Nothing great comes cheap. This stripping is working for you; your adversity reveals you. You will not be known only by your successes, but by how you overcome your obstacles. God has something a lot bigger than what happened to you yesterday. The Lord has such a plan for you. Continue to dream and let Him use you to heal others who are hurting.

> *It might look like the stripping locusts have eaten you alive, but God is a God of Restoration!*

> *And I will restore or replace for you the years that the locust has eaten—the hopping locust, the stripping locust, and the crawling locust, My great army which I sent among you. And you shall eat in plenty and be satisfied and praise the name of the Lord, your God, Who has dealt wondrously with you. And My people shall never be put to shame* (Joel 2:25-26 AMP).

You will recover and move on to God's purpose. Recovery can take many forms, so leave the finished work in His skilled hands. Get intoxicated with where you are going and refuse to be tied down to where you have been. We must live in the present and face our futures with a hope in Him. The past is behind us.

Whatever you need to face your tomorrows, God will provide it. Sometimes, we find His provision in the most unlikely places.

After my husband's death, praying and driving became a way to vent my pain. On one of my extremely long, lonely driving days, I turned my rental monster truck into the parking lot of a junk store. I was restless and hurting and lonely and quickly looked over the broken and scratched CDs for sale. I thought maybe I would find something that would help me during my desperate drives.

I found a two-CD series by a minister I'd never even heard of. The set was on sale; it was reduced to half price, discounted down from $6 to $3. I wasn't sure I was worth 12 quarters, but I thought maybe there would be something on these CDs—some word, some thought that would help me find a way to live again. I was just that desperate. I needed to find hope.

"Hallelu-lu-lu-lu-lu-lu-lu…" the preacher said. He had my attention, but the CD was so scratched, the message skipped and sputtered. Yet, somehow I sensed the Presence of God moving through my heart. For the next two hours, I was glued to every word and thought that this stranger conveyed. It seemed as though he had been watching my life for years.

I heard him tell about the trials of Abraham, and I heard him tell about the bumps in life's road and the shaky places that we sometimes find ourselves on. I could not believe what I was hearing. It was just like this man knew me and had watched my life free-fall for the previous five years. I wept uncontrollably. God had hooked an IV of hope directly into my spirit.

Then the Spirit of the Lord spoke to my heart. "Wherever this man is, find him, and listen to the words that I will give him for your life."

"You're kidding me, God. But I'm so desperate, I'm willing to try anything just to live!"

I could only hope that I heard the Lord right. Nervously, I called the number on the back of the CD cover. I got an answering machine. This discouraged me because I had called Dial-A-Prayer earlier, and the number had been disconnected. Oh brother! I didn't leave a message, because no one would have believed this crazy story.

Days later, on another prayer drive, I tried the number again. This time, I connected with a real human on the other end of the phone. I gave him the abbreviated version of the junk-store setup, and I asked where I could find and attend the next conference where this minister would be speaking. The administrator on the phone told me that the minister and his team would be in Atlanta, Georgia, in three months. Perfect! It took all the courage I could summon, but I made plans to meet the junk-store minister that had spoken words of life through this heavenly, scratched-up treasure.

Attending the conference in Atlanta was a last-ditch effort to see if God really had any hope for me. I felt like God had spoken clearly to me that this total stranger would have a word of hope for my life. True to the promptings of the Spirit of God, the minister singled me out of the meeting during the middle of the service. He asked if I would come to the front of the auditorium. Of course, I would. I wanted to live and not die. I would have climbed to the top of the Eiffel Tower if that had been the instruction. I was more than ready to hope again. I needed to raise my fatherless son, and I needed to see if there was really life on the other side of this bottomless pit.

Standing there in front of this man sent from God, he looked at me with compassion in his eyes. He spoke directly into my heart as everyone in attendance prayerfully rose to their feet.

"I don't know who you are, and I don't where you came from, and I don't know what you've been walking through," his voice rang with a sound of deliverance. "But God has sent you here to let you know that He is not through with you. It's time for you to get back in the game. Tonight is your recommissioning service!"

My spirit broke. The floodgates of Heaven had opened. God had spoken to me just like He did when I drove away from the junk store weeks earlier.

You are going to rise above it all. We cannot avoid the curves of life, but we don't have to be defined by them, either. God has a way for you to hope. You might not know that way right now, and you might not feel that it is within your reach, but He knows the way, and He has the plan. Tell all your senses to be on high alert. You are going to hope again.

God had designed and planned for Abraham to father a son (see Gen. 15:4). More than 20 years passed and still there was no son. Abraham's hope had been deferred because the promise seemed to be delayed. Yet, Abraham believed God and believed in hope against hope (see Rom. 4:18). Even when a death sentence had been placed upon his hope, he still found a way to hope (see Gen. 22:3).

When God makes a promise to our lives, it is not up to us to fulfill it. What God wants is our openness and submissiveness to His divine possibilities. Will you trust Him? Will you give Him your confidence? He doesn't need you to be the divine "fixer" in your life. He will be all that and more.

(As it is written, I have made thee a father of many nations,) before Him whom he believed, even God, who quickeneth the dead, and calleth those things which be not as though they were. Who against hope believed in hope, that he might become the father of many nations; according to that which was spoken, So shall thy seed be. And being not weak in faith, he considered not his own body now dead, when he was about an hundred years old, neither yet the deadness of Sarah's womb: he staggered not at the promise of God through unbelief; but was strong in faith, giving glory to God; and being fully persuaded that, what He had promised, He was able also to perform (Romans 4:17-21).

God is the One who is able. He is the One who has promised. He not only has intention; He has placed Himself within the boundaries of obligation.

Open Wounds, Open Doors

There is a real enemy. In the Bible, he is called many different titles and names. He is known as the prince of darkness and also beelzebub, the lord of the flies (see Matt. 12:24).[2]

It's deeper than you think.

I can understand these titles, for they are very descriptive of how I perceive this evil being. Almost everyone knows that flies are the dirtiest thing on this planet, and they cause more diseases than any other insect.

And He was casting out a devil, and it was dumb. And it came to pass, when the devil was gone out, the dumb spake; and the people wondered. But some of them said, He casteth out devils through Beelzebub the chief of the devils. And others, tempting Him, sought of Him a sign from heaven. But He, knowing their thoughts, said unto them, Every kingdom divided against itself is brought to desolation; and a house divided against a house falleth. If Satan also be divided against himself, how shall his kingdom stand? because ye say that I cast out devils through Beelzebub. And if I by Beelzebub cast out devils, by whom do your sons cast them out? Therefore shall they be your judges. But if I with the finger of God cast out devils, no doubt the kingdom of God is come upon you (Luke 11:14-20).

Beelzebub translated in the Greek means *"lord of the flies."* This name gives us insight into the nature of satan and tells us at least four things about the work of satan and his demons. As is the case with flies:

- They are carriers of disease.
- They breed quickly, given the right environment.
- They invade all territories.
- They are attracted to junk, garbage, and trash.

I have noticed while traveling in Africa on many mission trips that some tropical flies even lay eggs under the skin, giving birth to maggots that pop out of boils. This reminds me of the "hidden" flies, the hidden maladies that are deep within many wounded Christians.

If we have open wounds that have produced bitterness, resentment, revenge, and jealousies, we become breeding grounds of demonic activity.

If we have "junk" in our lives—the sins that we hold onto, the attitudes of which the Holy Spirit convicts us—we become places of demonic interest. Social, educational, or economic status does not prevent us from being infested. Flies are everywhere; *the rich, the poor, the ignorant, and the educated are all the same to flies!*

Is there some offense that you need to release? Is there something that you need to let go? Is there something that you need to leave behind? Is there a person that you need to forgive? Do you need to disconnect from the baggage of the past? Do you need to lay some things at the feet of Jesus and leave them there? Will you allow Him to convict you? Cleanse you? Heal you?

We must not allow ourselves to become lukewarm. Flies will avoid fire. The one area in which I have never seen a fly land in my home is in the fireplace. God's Word tells us to be burning, on fire, ablaze with the Holy Spirit's power in our lives.

> *I indeed baptize you with water unto repentance: but He that cometh after me is mightier than I, whose shoes I am not worthy to bear: He shall baptize you with the Holy Ghost, and with fire...* (Matthew 3:11).

> *So then because thou art lukewarm, and neither cold nor hot, I will spue thee out of My mouth* (Revelation 3:16).

> *Never lag in zeal and in earnest endeavor; be aglow and burning with the Spirit, serving the Lord* (Romans 12:11 AMP).

Ask Jesus to, once again, fill you with His Spirit. This is how we overcome. It is only through Him.

And they have overcome (conquered) him by means of the blood of the Lamb and by the utterance of their testimony... (Revelation 12:11 AMP).

Demonic spirits live in a realm of despair and hopelessness. Hopelessness is the emotion of hell. It is the permanent residence of despair, and it is the gravitational pull toward the heart of hell itself.

It has been said by some that a man can live 40 days without food, 3 days without water, 8 minutes without air, but not one second without hope. A person cannot live without hope.

Your season of gloom is coming to a rapid close in your life. Your trial has a time limit. Just as it had a beginning, it has a middle and an ending. The timer is running, and you are getting closer to a life filled with His amazing hopes restored.

No temptation has overtaken you but such as is common to man; and God is faithful, who will not allow you to be tempted beyond what you are able, but with the temptation will provide the way of escape also, that you may be able to endure it (1 Corinthians 10:13 NASB).

Hopelessness and despair might have been breeding grounds for oppressive spirits, but those days are over! It is time to lift up your head. When David was depressed, he learned to lift up his head. If you can look up, you can get up.

Lift up your heads, O ye gates; and be ye lift up, ye everlasting doors; and the King of glory shall come in (Psalm 24:7).

And now shall mine head be lifted up above mine enemies round about me: therefore will I offer in His tabernacle sacrifices of joy; I will sing, yea, I will sing praises unto the Lord (Psalm 27:6).

Walking in Your Ultimate Destiny

The trials of our lives are not designed to kill us. This cannot take you out. It is not your time to die. God is working a higher plan, a higher purpose than you can imagine. Just because you have walked through a chapter of hopelessness and despair, it doesn't mean your whole life is destined to be like that. Your life will not be defined by this dark night of the soul. Never does a single chapter of any book tell the whole story.

[You should] be exceedingly glad on this account, though now for a little while you may be distressed by trials and suffer temptations, So that [the genuineness] of your faith may be tested, [your faith] which is infinitely more precious than the perishable gold which is tested and purified by fire. [This proving of your faith is intended] to redound to [your] praise and glory and honor when Jesus Christ (the Messiah, the Anointed One) is revealed (1 Peter 1:6-7 AMP).

This testing is for your place and purpose in the Kingdom. God's glory is going to be revealed even in the middle of the fire.

You didn't just come to this planet to take up space and then to die. You have a purpose in life; you have a divine assignment. You might not know exactly what it is, and you might not know what your present trial has to do with all of this, but your enemy has perceived what is in your glorious future.

Is there a possibility that your future has purpose—an assignment from the Lord—that your enemy has discerned and recognized? Could it be that kingdoms of darkness are right now intimidated by the impact of your life? Like a palm tree, your roots are being dug deeply, so that your strength may rise higher and higher! You are destined to give many others hope!

It is not only what we presently are, but what we are becoming that attracts the attention of hell itself. When the adversary sees what God has invested in you, he, himself, knows that if you don't quit, you will walk in your ultimate destiny. The devil knows that if you don't quit, you will win, because Jesus has already provided the victory!

I have been on the floor, in the basement of life with all of the electricity turned off. Everything was crashing and falling apart. I have been there when all my hopes and dreams were dashed to the ground, and to me, life was no longer worth living. Some of you are about to give up, to throw in the towel, to quit, to walk away, to abandon your dream. That's why the Holy Spirit is sending this message of hope to you right now!

Your perspectives are already changing!

No, despite all these things, overwhelming victory is ours through Christ, who loved us (Romans 8:37 NLT).

Endnotes

1. Brennan Manning, *Ruthless Trust,* (San Francisco: Harper, 2000) 5-6.

2. "Baal-zebub." The Columbia Encyclopedia, Sixth Edition. 2008. Retrieved January 5, 2010, from Encyclopedia.com: http://www. encyclopedia.com/doc/1E1-Baalzebu.html.

Hope Journal

_____
_____
_____
_____
_____
_____
_____
_____
_____
_____
_____
_____
_____
_____
_____
_____
_____
_____
_____
_____
_____
_____

Hope
Journal

Hope
Journal

CHAPTER THREE

This Is Bigger Than You

I'm not saying that I have this all together, that I have it made. But I am well on my way, reaching out for Christ, who has so wondrously reached out for me. Friends, don't get me wrong: By no means do I count myself an expert in all of this, but I've got my eye on the goal, where God is beckoning us onward—to Jesus. I'm off and running, and I'm not turning back (Philippians 3:12-14 MSG).

When you were a newborn, you never even thought about driving a car. You didn't know that cars existed. In the same way, when we first come to know the Lord by the blood of Jesus Himself, we are new in the faith. We have no idea or concept of the processes of our lives and what the formation of our future even looks like. When we are born again, we start a new life, a life that connects to a higher cause and purpose.

It is just as when we are newborn babies and we connect to the world outside of our mother's womb. Even so, now that we are born again, we connect to the life of God and to all the purposes of the Kingdom of God in our lives, even when we do not know or understand what that might be or what it might mean. We never seem to have a grip or perfect understanding of all of His Kingdom purposes. We are called to trust the process.

My mother learned this as a young parent. Because of my dad's Air Force travels, our family was temporarily stationed near Chicago. On a particular day at a downtown laundromat, Mom had put me on the table in a little baby carry-all. She turned to get some laundry, looked back, and I was gone.

My three-year-old brother cried out, "Momma, Chitchy gone! Momma, Chitchy gone!" He could barely reach the hem of my mother's dress at the time. I was only three months old. Mother screamed in response to my big brother's plea. She screamed out for help, saying, "My baby's gone! Somebody took my baby!"

Within seconds, she and the manager of the business darted out the side door with my little brother running on their heels. Instinctively, they ran for the long back alley behind the laundromat. As they approached the darkened alleyway, they saw a frail, grubby, dirty elderly woman with an old rotten onion sack in one hand and me in the other one.

Fearful for my life, Mom stared into the woman's eyes for several awkward seconds before speaking. "I want my baby back," Mom begged.

"I've always wanted a baby like this," the woman responded.

"But that's my baby; I want my baby back," Mom persisted.

Afraid that this kidnapper would hurl me to the pavement or cut me with a knife or injure me in some way, my mother waited as intense seconds passed by. Hesitantly, the woman handed me to Mom. The manager then told Mom that a mentally challenged woman had been stalking the children at this place of business for quite some time.

Just like He watches over the little sparrows, He watched over me.

Are not two sparrows sold for a farthing? and one of them shall not fall on the ground without your Father. But the very hairs of your head are all numbered. Fear ye not therefore, ye are of more value than many sparrows (Matthew 10:29-31).

As I grew up, hearing my own mother tell me that story over and over, I knew God had His hand on me. Only He knows what would have happened to my life, if that deranged woman had ever turned the corner in that Chicago back alley.

Somehow, being a victim of a failed kidnap attempt has helped to anchor me in times of adversity. If God delivered me then, could He not deliver me now? If God had a purpose for saving me then, was I not worth saving now? If God cared for me then, did He not care for me now? If God had hope for me then, doesn't He have hope for me now?

Looking back, this was another lesson of His faithfulness. He could testify to me of His faithfulness, even before I knew that I needed Him to be faithful. There is always a bigger picture and His plan is bigger than all of us could ever imagine.

Nothing happens by accident. We must understand that we all have purpose, that our lives are now connected to the Kingdom of God. It sounds almost comical, but the purpose of life is *purpose.* We all have an assignment. It is like the Greek athletes who were each given a lane to run in. You have your lane and I have mine. My assignment is not the same as yours, and yours is not the same as mine. We are unique. *We are each one of a kind!*

There is no need to want to be like someone else. We don't need to covet another person's anointing or calling. You don't know the price they paid to walk in that type of anointing and Presence of God upon their lives. Accept your assignment. Even if that means the preparations that you will walk through are painful and hard. God has not promised that our skies would always be blue. If you don't quit, you will make it through this season of your life.

Refuse to be distracted. Stay in your lane. Understand that the rigorous training is part of your destiny to give others hope. You are going to impact lives for the glory of God. Keep pressing for the prize.

Why So Pressed?

In the Old Testament, those things that were going to be used in the service of the sanctuary had to be anointed with oil. Once they were anointed, they were set apart, sanctified, and ready for use. Also, prophets, priests, and kings were anointed for service. This anointing oil is described in the book of Exodus.

> *Moreover the Lord spake unto Moses, saying, Take thou also unto thee principal spices, of pure myrrh five hundred shekels, and of sweet cinnamon half so much, even two hundred and fifty shekels,*

and of sweet calamus two hundred and fifty shekels, and of cassia five hundred shekels, after the shekel of the sanctuary, and of oil olive an hin: and thou shalt make it an oil of holy ointment, an ointment compound after the art of the apothecary: it shall be an holy anointing oil (Exodus 30:22-25).

The ingredients had to be processed and carefully measured. Interestingly, one of the five ingredients was myrrh. Myrrh is very bitter. Have you ever wondered why bitter experiences are a part of your life? Have you ever spent sleepless nights wondering why? It's because of the anointing; He is creating a special spice. Your life will become a fragrance poured out.

To make anointing oil, the myrrh had to be measured. Exactly 500 shekels of myrrh were needed. Why? Because myrrh was measured by weight, and the weight of God's presence, influence, and power are destined to flow through your life—sometimes not in spite of, but because of, the bitter places that God has allowed you to walk through.

The very thing that the enemy thought would take you out, is the thing that is pressing the oil of God's anointing into and through your life. Trust God radically!

There could be no anointing oil without myrrh.

This anointing process is going to be the catalyst that will accelerate your purpose. There is no need for anointing if you have no purpose. Why should God anoint you, for no reason? The oil will not be wasted.

This pressing of your life will not be in vain. You will have substance because of this. You are not a microwave believer. You have been pressed and formed by the Master. You will arise from this place to fulfill your assignment in the Kingdom of God. Your story is not over.

You will carry out your assignment because of the anointing in and upon your life.

...I shall be anointed with fresh oil (Psalm 92:10).

It is this anointing that will give you such a resolve that you will never cave in during times of extreme difficulty. You will carry such a purpose that you will dance on the ashes of the ruins of your life and you will give God a radical praise, even when you do not understand why everything happened the way that it did. You will live to see your life turned around. God will never waste one bitter experience. He will give you beauty if you will give Him your ashes.

> *To appoint unto them that mourn in Zion, to give unto them **beauty** for **ashes**, the oil of joy for mourning, the garment of praise for the spirit of heaviness; that they might be called trees of righteousness, the planting of the Lord, that He might be glorified* (Isaiah 61:3).

Storms, Storms, and More Storms

The storms of our lives can become indicators, signposts of change. Just as signs alert the driver that construction is ahead, demolition can also indicate that something new is coming. In December 2004 and in August 2005, two similar disasters hit our world. The Asian tsunami, which took about 250,000 souls into eternity, and Hurricane Katrina, the fierce visitor that left a footprint in the southeastern United States, changed forever the surrounding landscapes.

The tsunami came without warning. A single event devastated large areas of coastline. In a similar way, New Orleans, Louisiana, became a toxic soup bowl in the course of a single day. In both cases, many lives were affected and changed by just one circumstance.

We cannot choose our storms, but we can choose our building materials. God will use events of our lives to build strength in us so that we have endurance. The amazing power to endure comes from sitting at the feet of Jesus. He will give you endurance for the race. Sometimes you don't have to be the fastest runner, just the one who will not quit.

> *We pray that you'll have the strength to stick it out over the long haul—not the grim strength of gritting your teeth but the glory-strength God gives. It is strength that endures the unendurable and spills over into joy, thanking the Father who makes us strong enough to take part in everything bright and beautiful that He has for us* (Colossians 1:11-12 MSG).

Most often, it is the pressures and the struggles of life that do more to strengthen us than the times of ease and little resistance. We really are strengthened through the struggle.

It is like the little bird fighting to come out of its shell. The push actually forms the bird. If a person were to try and rescue the tiny struggling creature, it would actually be deformed for life, unable to fly, and consequently, unable to achieve its purpose in life.

When you are struggling, be patient and hold on to God's reliable hand. He forges His chosen vessels in the place of pressure. The difference in your life will be the foundation that you have laid. Have you trusted Christ and Christ alone as your Rock? When everything else has crashed, do you still stand on Him and on Him alone? Your friends may walk out, you may bury your loved ones, your money may not last, your network or your net worth may be shifting; but upon what kind of foundation have you built your life?

> *He only is my rock and my salvation: He is my defence; I shall not be moved* (Psalm 62:6).

> *According to the grace of God which is given unto me, as a wise master builder, I have laid the foundation, and another buildeth thereon. But let every man take heed how he buildeth thereupon. For other foundation can no man lay than that is laid, which is Jesus Christ* (1 Corinthians 3:10-11).

> *For in the time of trouble He shall hide me in His pavilion: in the secret of His tabernacle shall He hide me; He shall set me up upon a rock* (Psalm 27:5).

Any house that is built upon rock will withstand storms. You will also stand firmly during this time of trial if your feet are planted firmly upon the Rock, Christ Jesus.

> *And the rain descended, and the floods came, and the winds blew, and beat upon that house; and it **fell not**: for it was founded upon a rock* (Matthew 7:25).

Sometimes storms come and contradict everything that you ever thought about the direction of your life. When your heart is torn apart and everything is seemingly contrary to the blessings of God upon your life, you will have to square back your shoulders and trust that you are standing on the Rock. You will have to remind yourself that, even though life may move, this Rock will never move.

Crisis and chaos look and feel like sure signs that your world is upside down, yet they are about to become the incubators of your miracle. This is important, because storms will come. There are six main ways in which you will face trying storms:

Spiritually…

Physically…

Mentally…

Relationally…

Financially…

In your destiny.

It would be easy to think that life is composed only of storms; but never believe it. Storms do come, but they eventually go. They are only part of life's changing weather. Not every day will be like this one. Things will change.

I have been given a mandate from God, an assignment that is so clear. My call is to encourage and empower you right now, today, right in the middle of your storm. I have buried my loved ones while I was fighting my way through my own personal tsunami. I can tell you, your life is not over. God will use all of the events of your life to transform you for His glory. When my husband, the love of my life, died in my arms, I had to understand that my hope was not in Bill, but in Christ alone.

David said it beautifully:

Unto You, O Lord, do I bring my life. O my God, I trust, lean on, rely on, and am confident in You. Let me not be put to shame or [my hope in You] be disappointed... (Psalm 25:1-2 AMP).

My hopes could no longer be in my husband. He had been promoted to a "heavenly grandstand." The time had come for me to rely totally upon God's unfailing love.

I have learned by experience that if you have lost something in life, surrender all to Him, because He is planning and orchestrating a glorious future beyond your comprehension. Even though you do not understand it all, you can trust the One who created you and formed you and chose you before the world began.

Even as [in His love] He chose us [actually picked us out for Himself as His own] in Christ before the foundation of the world, that we should be holy (consecrated and set apart for Him) and blameless in His sight, even above reproach, before Him in love. For He foreordained us (destined us, planned in love for us) to be adopted (revealed) as His own children through Jesus Christ, in accordance with the purpose of His will [because it pleased Him and was His kind intent]... (Ephesians 1:4-5 AMP).

A Wind You Cannot Control

The apostle Paul was caught in a ferocious storm at sea. The event is described in the Book of Acts, chapter 27. As overwhelming as the storm seemed to be, Paul was about to defy all odds.

*Now when much time was spent, and when sailing was now dangerous, because the fast was now already past, Paul admonished them, and said unto them, Sirs, I perceive that this voyage will be with hurt and much damage, not only of the lading and ship, but also of our lives. Nevertheless the centurion believed the master and the owner of the ship, more than those things which were spoken by Paul. And because the haven was not commodious to winter in, the more part advised to depart thence also, if by any means they might attain to Phenice, and there to winter; which is an haven of Crete, and lieth toward the south west and north west. And when the south wind blew softly, supposing that they had obtained their purpose, loosing thence, they sailed close by Crete. But not long after there arose against it a tempestuous wind, called Euroclydon. And when the ship was caught, and could not bear up into the wind, we let her drive. And running under a certain island which is called Clauda, we had much work to come by the boat: which when they had taken up, they used helps, undergirding the ship; and, fearing lest they should fall into the quicksands, strake sail, and so were driven. And we being exceedingly tossed with a tempest, the next day they lightened the ship; and the third day we cast out with our own hands the tackling of the ship. **And when neither sun nor stars in many days appeared, and no small***

tempest lay on us, all hope that we should be saved was then taken away. But after long abstinence Paul stood forth in the midst of them, and said, Sirs, ye should have hearkened unto me, and not have loosed from Crete, and to have gained this harm and loss. And now I exhort you to be of good cheer: for there shall be no loss of any man's life among you, but of the ship. For there stood by me this night the angel of God, whose I am, and whom I serve, saying, Fear not, Paul; thou must be brought before Caesar: and, lo, God hath given thee all them that sail with thee. Wherefore, sirs, be of good cheer: for I believe God, that it shall be even as it was told me. Howbeit we must be cast upon a certain island. But when the fourteenth night was come, as we were driven up and down in Adria, about midnight the shipmen deemed that they drew near to some country; and sounded, and found it twenty fathoms: and when they had gone a little further, they sounded again, and found it fifteen fathoms. Then fearing lest we should have fallen upon rocks, they cast four anchors out of the stern, and wished for the day. And as the shipmen were about to flee out of the ship, when they had let down the boat into the sea, under colour as though they would have cast anchors out of the foreship, Paul said to the centurion and to the soldiers, Except these abide in the ship, ye cannot be saved. Then the soldiers cut off the ropes of the boat, and let her fall off. And while the day was coming on, Paul besought them all to take meat, saying, This day is the fourteenth day that ye have tarried and continued fasting, having taken nothing. Wherefore I pray you to take some meat: for this is for your health: for there shall not an hair fall from the head of any of you. And when he had thus spoken, he took bread, and gave thanks to God in presence of them *all: and when he had broken it, he began to eat. Then were they all of good cheer, and they also took some meat. And we were in all in the ship two hundred threescore and sixteen souls. And when they had eaten enough, they lightened the ship, and cast out the wheat into the sea. And when it was day, they knew not the land: but they discovered a certain creek with a shore, into the which they were minded, if it were possible, to thrust in the ship. And when they had taken up the anchors, they committed themselves unto the sea, and loosed the rudder bands, and hoised up the mainsail to the wind, and made toward shore. And falling into a place where two seas met, they ran the ship aground; and the forepart stuck fast, and remained unmoveable, but the hinder part was broken with the violence of the waves* (Acts 27:9-41).

Emphasized here, verse 20 gives us a strong indication of the devastating effects of this storm. To a sailor, if you have no sun or stars, you have no direction or bearings because you have no compass points from which to navigate. Yet the Bible tells us that these were the conditions Paul and his traveling companions experienced for many days. They were caught in a storm that could not be controlled.

You might be in such a storm now—one that seems to have you in its grip. Your options are limited, but you are not without hope, even when it seems that all hope is gone. Guess what? A storm like that is the perfect time for God's power to sweep into your situation and salvage your life from the wreckage.

Paul went to prayer. He understood that prayer is the breeding ground for hope. Prayer is the environment in which hope can grow. It is the communication through which we are reminded of God's presence, power, and love.

He will fulfill the desire of them that fear Him: He also will hear their cry, and will save them (Psalm 145:19).

But they that wait upon the Lord shall renew their strength; they shall mount up with wings as eagles; they shall run, and not be weary; and they shall walk, and not faint (Isaiah 40:31).

I know you might not feel like praying, but this is the very time that you need to pray. If you are walking through the ferocious storms of life, it is time to pray. Prayer will be the oxygen that prevents you from drowning. Now is the exact time to lock yourself in the prayer closet and seek Him. Fall on your knees and diligently cry out to God.

There is a cry that God cannot deny. Has He heard that cry from you? There is much to be said about crying when you are crying out to God. There's enough crying over who left, who's not coming back, what you lost, what you thought you needed, what you thought you deserved and never got. There's enough of that. You can keep crying, but it's time to change what you are crying about. Now is the time to cry out for God to touch you, heal you, make you whole, direct you, assign people to your life, and cause you to *hope again.*

…The rock of my strength, my refuge is in God.…Pour out your heart before Him; God is a refuge for us (Psalm 62:7-8 NASB).

Before Paul prayed, it seemed everything would be lost. After he prayed, Paul had a message of hope. Prayer changes your perspective about your trial. It changes your view of the storm. So many times, we have been told to not ask God "Why?" But, rest assured, God can handle your *why*. Prayer positions your spirit away from the natural circumstances and onto the promises of God's Word. We'll get back to more about Paul and this storm a little later. Just remember these words of Jesus:

These things I have spoken unto you, that in Me ye might have peace. In the world ye shall have tribulation: but be of good cheer; I have overcome the world (John 16:33).

Gandhi once said: "It is better in prayer to have a heart without words, than words without heart." When your heart is breaking and your hope has taken sleeping pills, it is hard to articulate words. That's OK, too, because God understands. He knows the expression of your very breath.

After losing Bill, I cried out to Him, saying, "God, I have no more words." I moaned through my tears. I was up to my neck in the hot waters of pain, and things were not getting better. My hopes were lost, and my dreams had been shattered.

I spent most of my days screaming and crying uncontrollably. On a certain day, I headed out the door for another one of my screaming prayer drives. I asked, "Lord, are You with me or not?"

I needed to feel His Presence; I needed for Him to restore me. I needed His assistance to even pray. Just as I reached for the kitchen door-knob and prepared to leave the house, I felt a very slight inward nudge. Suddenly, I had a faint impression in my heart: *Take your shofar when you go out to pray today.* I quickly grabbed the ram's horn that a friend had brought me from Israel years before. I didn't know why I was to take my shofar, but I did experience a sense of the Lord Himself being involved in this instruction.

As I turned the ignition of my vehicle, and grabbed the steering wheel tightly, I screamed out, "God, what is happening? I don't know anything else to say to You." I had been honestly crying out to God with every word that I knew to say. I was depleted from all the heartrending and gut-wrenching tragedies I had experienced.

As I drove, my emotions rose and fell like tidal waves. I sensed that I should pull over to the side of the road and blow the shofar. The ram's horn is hard to blow and requires much breath to create a sound. I think it was God's way of letting my breath praise Him. Didn't He say, *"Let everything that hath breath, praise the Lord"* (Ps. 150:6)?

I recalled the Old Testament sounding of the shofar. Amazing things happened when the shofar was blown. I wasn't sure what this had to do with me, but I was willing to become a spectacle on the roadside. I was willing to try *anything* that might restore my hope!

Pulling off to the side of a major highway, I opened the door and began to blow my shofar like there was no tomorrow. My whole body turned blood red with each difficult blast. It felt as though the veins on my neck had popped out like sausage links. Somehow, maybe He would take my breath and begin to replace it with His breath. I cannot begin to imagine what passing motorists must have thought. All I know is that I wanted to live, and I needed Him to breathe hope into my soul.

Habakkuk the prophet asked:

How long, O Lord, must I call for help, but You do not listen?…
[God answered,] *"…watch—and be utterly amazed. For I am*
going to do something in your days that you would not believe, even
if you were told" (Habakkuk 1:2,5 NIV).

I have been qualified in the furnace of affliction to tell you that the
Holy Spirit is our Helper; He's *your* Helper. The Holy Spirit is the "breath
of God." When God made the first man, Adam, He breathed into him
the breath of life (see Gen. 2:7).

…We know not what we should pray for as we ought: but the Spirit
itself maketh intercession for us with groanings which cannot be
uttered (Romans 8:26).

…He breathed on them and said, "Receive the Holy Spirit…"
(John 20:22 NIV).

Now is the time to understand the power of the Holy Spirit and His
enablement in prayer. If you will engage the heart, at this time, the Spirit
of God will take it from there. Simple obedience empowers hope. From
this position of humility and brokenness before Him, you will spiritually
assimilate the hope that the Spirit of Hope will begin to gently nourish
into your life.

Therefore everyone who hears these words of Mine, and acts upon
them, may be compared to a wise man, who built his house upon
the rock. And the rain descended, and the floods came, and the
winds blew, and burst against that house; and yet it did not fall, for
it had been founded upon the rock (Matthew 7:24-25 NASB).

Before we go on, let's briefly review some key points discussed so far:

- The God Zone is the place where you acknowledge that God is real, and you must connect with Him.

- The place of prayer is the most significant place of your life.

- Your trial is working for you.

- Remember to close every oppressive door that was opened by an emotional wound.

- The challenges of your life have purpose.

- The anointing increases when you properly respond to pressure.

- Storms are signposts that indicate change.

Hope
Journal

Hope
Journal

CHAPTER FOUR

Expectation Is a Law

Serial disappointments can land anyone in an emotional crater. Unchecked, life's letdowns can convince us that the future will be framed by disappointment, too.

Unmet expectations can create some of our most tender emotional bruises. For example, psychologists will tell you that when you are not affirmed by someone who should affirm you (a parent, for instance), you are likely to suffer one of the most harmful emotional wounds in life.

When this happens, we begin to erect façades because we don't want anybody to know just how injured we are. Often, we are embarrassed when those who should affirm us fail to do so. We wish so deeply that things could have been different.

Even when we maintain the pretense that we are OK, inwardly we are crying for rescue. We simply do not want to bear these kinds of scars in our lives.

Sometimes others wound us; sometimes we wound ourselves. Sometimes it is both. Either way, we need healing from the emotional damage of unmet expectations resulting from affirmation that was needed, but withheld.

What are you carrying around that is too weighty for you? Is it disappointment? Regret? Fear? Abuse? What has taken your peace like a thief in the night? A broken home? Abusive relationships? Loss of loved ones through death, abandonment, or rejection? Opportunities that have been lost?

Your dreams can live again. Your abilities can soar again. *You can hope again!* Your unresolved hurts are an opportunity for God to move. You are being assisted in your return journey to positive expectations.

H.O.P.E.—Rebuild Your Broken Life

Having Optimistic Positive Expectations

Now is the time to build and rebuild. Your life is not over. There is new hope for you. Even if you have lost years, they have not been lost to God. God is the Creator and Redeemer of time. He is in the restoring business.

> *And I will restore or replace for you the years that the locust has eaten—the hopping locust, the stripping locust, and the crawling locust...* (Joel 2:25 AMP).

Many times, restoration is not exactly what you think it is. Your dreams might not be exactly as they once were. Your hopes might take a different perspective. Lost years might come back in a different form. You might need a new definition of normal as He rebuilds and restores your life. For example, when a spouse dies, the life you had as a family dies. My son and I had to find a new life, a new way of normal living. New dreams began to emerge. When you make God your partner, you let Him restore you His way for His purposes with His hopes.

The law of expectation must be solidly grounded in the finished work of Christ Jesus. I can expect again because of what He did for me. I can hope again because of the inestimable price that Jesus Christ paid. He not only gives hope, He is our hope! This is a non-negotiable law of God. Jesus paid it all.

"Lord, I've had so many losses. I've lost this, and I've lost that, and I've lost them," I moaned, prayerfully reflecting on the losses I'd suffered in a short period of time.

I felt His tender compassion, and then I heard Him speak to my heart, "But you've still got Me." He remained true to me, in spite of my bitter tears. My life of brokenness, heartache, and disappointments could still look at the empty cross and realize that nobody was beyond the reach of that kind of love.

I have no patented formulas to offer. But there is a strength of expectation when it is foundationally based on the gift of Christ Jesus. I want to share with you what I believe to be the very basic fundamental building block on your journey back to hope.

I am going to make a hope statement that I want you to repeat aloud and make a part of your daily life.

The Strength of My Position Is Always in Christ.

Here are some Scriptures to pore over daily, saying them aloud, until your hope begins to soar again. They describe the many facets of life in Christ, and they remind us that believers have a nonnegotiable position of hope and value in Him! He is our identity!

What Does Being "in Christ" Mean?

As you consider these Scriptures, allow them to build within you a sense of who you really are, *in Him.*

I am sanctified (made holy) in Jesus Christ
(1 Corinthians 1:2).

I am pure, holy, and saved in Christ
(1 Corinthians 1:30 TLB).

I am a laborer together with God
(1 Corinthians 3:9).

I am daily overcoming the devil
(1 John 4:4).

I am healed by His stripes
(1 Peter 2:24).

I am casting all my care on Jesus
(1 Peter 5:7).

I am blessed with spiritual weapons and am casting down vain imaginations
(2 Corinthians 10:4-5).

I am bringing every thought into captivity
(2 Corinthians 10:5).

I am not moved by what I see
(2 Corinthians 4:18).

I am a new creation
(2 Corinthians 5:17).

I am made right with God
(2 Corinthians 5:21).

I am walking by faith and not by sight
(2 Corinthians 5:7).

I am a partaker of His divine nature
(2 Peter 1:4).

I have and share salvation with eternal glory
(2 Timothy 2:10).

I am delivered from the powers of darkness
(Colossians 1:13).

I am forgiven
(Colossians 1:14).

I am made complete in Christ
(Colossians 2:10).

I am set free from my sinful nature
(Colossians 2:11).

I am above only and not beneath
(Deuteronomy 28:13).

I am blessed coming in and blessed going out
(Deuteronomy 28:6).

I am an heir of eternal life
(1 John 2:25).

I am observing and doing the Lord's commandments
(Deuteronomy 28:13).

I am sealed with the Holy Spirit of promise
(Ephesians 1:13).

I am blessed with all spiritual blessings in Christ
(Ephesians 1:3).

I am holy and without blame
(Ephesians 1:4).

I am adopted as God's child
(Ephesians 1:5).

I am chosen by God
(Ephesians 1:4).

I am accepted in the Beloved
(Ephesians 1:6).

I am redeemed through His blood
(Ephesians 1:7).

I am God's masterpiece
(Ephesians 2:10).

I belong to Christ Jesus
(Ephesians 2:13).

I have been brought near to God
(Ephesians 2:13).

I am one with Christ
(Ephesians 2:6).

I am raised up to sit with Christ in the heavenly places
(Ephesians 2:6).

I am saved by grace through faith
(Ephesians 2:8).

I can come boldly and confidently into God's presence
(Ephesians 3:12).

I share in the promise of blessings through Christ
(Ephesians 3:6).

I am an imitator of Jesus
(Ephesians 5:1).

I am a member of Christ's Body, the Church
(Ephesians 5:29-30).

I am strong in the Lord and in the power of His might
(Ephesians 6:10).

I am redeemed from the curse of the law
(Galatians 3:13).

I am one in Christ with all other believers
(Galatians 3:28).

I am loving
(Galatians 5:22).

I am joyful
(Galatians 5:22).

I am peaceful
(Galatians 5:22).

Expectation Is a Law

I am patient
(Galatians 5:22).

I am kind
(Galatians 5:22).

I am good
(Galatians 5:22).

I am faithful
(Galatians 5:22).

I am gentle
(Galatians 5:23).

I have authority over all the power of the enemy
(Luke 10:19).

My name is recorded in Heaven
(Luke 10:20).

I establish God's Word on earth
(Matthew 16:19).

I am the salt and light of the world
(Matthew 5:13-14).

I can do all things through Christ who strengthens me
(Philippians 4:13).

I receive all my needs met by Christ Jesus
(Philippians 4:19).

I am redeemed from the hand of the enemy
(Psalm 107:2).

I am blessing and continually praising the Lord
(Psalm 34:1).

I abide under the shadow of the Almighty
(Psalm 91:1).

I am an overcomer by the blood of the Lamb
(Revelation 12:11).

I am being transformed by the renewing of my mind
(Romans 12:1-2).

I am not living under condemnation
(Romans 8:1).

I am led by the Spirit of God
(Romans 8:14).

I am a child of God
(Romans 8:16).

I am an heir of God and a joint-heir with Jesus
(Romans 8:17).

I am more than a conqueror
(Romans 8:37).

I am alive to God
(Romans 6:11).

I am free from the law of sin and death
(Romans 8:2).

I am walking in grace, favor, and spiritual blessing in
Christ Jesus
(1 Corinthians 1:4 AMP).

I am always led to triumph in Christ
(2 Corinthians 2:14).

I am pressing toward the goal to win in Christ Jesus
(Philippians 3:14).

Now complete healing can begin. God has a way of redeeming the losses in your life. Jesus did not come to patch you up; He came to make you new. Just as there has been deconstruction, reconstruction now begins.

He is looking for people who cannot free themselves from their pits. The reason we are delivered is because of what Jesus Christ has already done for us. The strength of our position is always in Christ.

The Spirit of the Lord [is] upon Me, because He has anointed Me
[the Anointed One, the Messiah] to preach the good news (the

Gospel) to the poor; He has sent Me to announce release to the captives and recovery of sight to the blind, to send forth as delivered those who are oppressed [who are downtrodden, bruised, crushed, and broken down by calamity]... (Luke 4:18 AMP).

If you have been broken down through calamities, your situation is perfect for God! Jesus is anointed for exactly what you think is impossible. If you will just allow Him and get out of the way, He can handle this whole situation.

To grant [consolation and joy] to those who mourn in Zion—to give them an ornament (a garland or diadem) of beauty instead of ashes, the oil of joy instead of mourning, the garment [expressive] of praise instead of a heavy, burdened, and failing spirit—that they may be called oaks of righteousness [lofty, strong, and magnificent, distinguished for uprightness, justice, and right standing with God], the planting of the Lord, that He may be glorified (Isaiah 61:3 AMP).

He really will give you beauty for ashes from a burned-out life!

In the Bible, the Holy Spirit and the Word of God are very sensitive and tender to hurting people. Our emotional wounds and bruises are just as real as the physical ones, but the hurt they cause us is far greater. Jesus is closely acquainted with what you are going through. He understands your struggles and is always moved with compassion.

He was despised and rejected and forsaken by men, a Man of sorrows and pains, and acquainted with grief and sickness; and like One from Whom men hide their faces He was despised, and we did not appreciate His worth or have any esteem for Him (Isaiah 53:3 AMP).

For we do not have a High Priest Who is unable to understand and sympathize and have a shared feeling with our weaknesses and infirmities and liability to the assaults of temptation, but One Who has been tempted in every respect as we are, yet without sinning (Hebrews 4:15 AMP).

Jesus knows and is completely familiar with:

- Abandonment
- Misunderstanding
- Rejection
- Betrayal
- Denial
- Abuse
- Shame
- Hurt
- Loss
- Humanity

God is making a "hope connection" with you now through Jesus Christ. He affirms you, validates you, and heals you. You will never shock God by the "mess" of your life, and your storms will never catch God off guard. He chose you before you walked in any decision-making ability for your life. That tells me, that whatever is needed, He has already gone before us to make the provisions necessary. It has already been released from Heaven. God does not change His mind about us because we walk through the valleys of life. He has already made every provision for your peace and assignments in this life.

Let Him speak to the broken place. Let Him come into the place that you have barricaded. Let Him work wholeness and recovery in your life. God has not changed His mind about your destiny—no matter what.

God's first intention about you is His final decision!

The gavel is down; the verdict is in; you belong to Him, and He is calling you out.

Today, He is calling you out of the struggle. He is freeing you from pain. It is time to let it all go. Don't give up on breakthrough now. Jesus Christ, the Truth is, even now, making you free.

See Beyond Where You Are Now

In the Gospels (see Mark 5; Luke 8), there is a story of a little girl who tragically died. She had all the budding hopes and promising aspirations of life ahead of her; yet she died. Her distraught father ran to Jesus with word of her sickness. While he was on his way to Jesus, she died.

But do you know what Jesus did? Jesus came anyway. Her story was not over. She was dead when Jairus got to Jesus, but Jesus went to her room anyhow. Some of you have already buried your once-growing dreams; you have already covered over the last bit of hope you had.

That's all right, because there is an anointing in the Holy Spirit now to *"hope you up."* Jesus comes to your situations even when they are already dead. He made a final decision about your life before you were born, and He is not about to change His mind just because of your present circumstances! Your situation is perfect for Him. What He needs now is your cooperation.

Now that you have established a firm belief in the God Zone, it is time to understand that the process of restoration and belief in the destiny of God has already been activated. Issues such as unforgiveness, bitterness, revenge, worry-filled living, and strife can now come under the covering of the blood of Jesus. This frees you to move into a life of clear, positive expectations rather than negative ones blurred by misplaced hopes or unmet expectations.

Unmet or misplaced expectations can lead our lives in the wrong direction. The process is subtle, but consequential. When expectations are not met, hope dwindles.

Now faith is the substance of things hoped for, the evidence of things not seen (Hebrews 11:1).

Hope is the springboard of our faith. Without hope, faith sputters and dies. So many times, we feel that the answer to our problems is to have more faith. We are even told, "Well, if you just have faith." Sometimes, we experience condemnation because it is assumed by others that we don't have faith. Others observe us from a limited viewpoint; they lack a complete understanding of our devastations. Yes, we are people of faith, but what about hope?

Some have wrongly analyzed the dilemma. Years ago, my son ran down the hallway of our home shouting, "Momma, Momma get in here quick! The dog's got termites!"

I was already halfway through the house when I stopped, falling to the floor with laughter. The dog did not have termites; the dog had fleas. My son knew there was a problem; he had simply misdiagnosed it.

Aren't we just like that? We often diagnose our problems as being rooted in a lack of faith when, in reality, it is our hopes that have been damaged.

How can we cry out for faith if we have lost hope? Hope must be restored. It is the Velcro that fastens our faith. Without hope, faith has nothing to which it can attach itself.

We often suffer "hope damage" because we have looked to people instead of God. Even on our best days, it is always time to focus our expectations on God.

David knew that nobody but God could meet his expectations.

My soul, wait thou only upon God; for my expectation is from Him. He only is my rock and my salvation: He is my defence; I shall not be moved. In God is my salvation and my glory: the rock of my strength, and my refuge, is in God. Trust in Him at all times; ye people, pour out your heart before Him: God is a refuge for us. Selah (Psalm 62:5-8).

David knew that mere man could neither deliver nor save him. Go back to your first love. Go back to the place you knew the Lord in pureness. Go back to the simple times when there was no support system, no people to disappoint you, no gains and no losses, but you had Him. Many things might have changed in your life, but you still have Him. There is great promise for you if you are still on this hope journey. The fact that you are here right now is the promise of renewed hope. You have a lot to work with from right where you are now.

It all began with Him anyway. Now, shift the focus back to Him. Run to the place of refuge and safety in Him. He will never fail you, and He will always be there to encourage you. He will be your hiding place when life hurts.

My soul, wait thou only upon God; for my expectation is from Him. He only is my rock and my salvation: He is my defence; I shall not be moved (Psalm 62:5-6).

He is your refuge when everything is in ruins.

In God is my salvation and my glory: the rock of my strength, and my refuge, is in God. Trust in Him at all times; ye people, pour out your heart before Him: God is a refuge for us. Selah (Psalm 62:7-8).

Whatever your situation, you can rely on God!

Hope
Journal

_____

_____

_____

_____

_____

_____

_____

_____

_____

_____

_____

_____

_____

_____

_____

_____

_____

_____

_____

_____

_____

_____

_____

_____

*Hope
Journal*

Hope Journal

CHAPTER FIVE

Out-of-Control Situations

Your Ziklag Moment

One of the most powerful stories of overcoming severe tragedy can be found in the Old Testament story of David at Ziklag (see 1 Sam. 30).

Ziklag was a Philistine town in which David and his men took refuge. Once, while David and his army were away, the Amalekites attacked and ravaged Ziklag, abducting the women and children and burning the entire city.

When David and his men returned to their base, they saw something they were in no way prepared to see. The magnitude of the disaster was evident: Their camp was destroyed, and their families were missing. As heartbroken husbands and fathers, they stood in the middle of the smoking ruins and wept until they could weep no more. It was the worst day of David's life.

*Now when David and his men came home to Ziklag on the third
day, they found that the Amalekites had made a raid on the South
(the Negeb) and on Ziklag, and had struck Ziklag and burned it
with fire, and had taken the women and all who were there, both
great and small, captive. They killed no one, but carried them off
and went on their way. So David and his men came to the town,
and behold, it was burned, and their wives and sons and daughters were taken captive. Then David and the men with him lifted
up their voices and wept until they had no more strength to weep*
(1 Samuel 30:1-4 AMP).

This could have been the place where David would succumb to the
sorrows of life. If ever there had been a way for the enemy to take out
David's purpose and destiny fulfillment, this would have been it.

To make matters worse, David's own men, the men that he loved,
turned their backs on him and threatened to stone their leader.

*David was greatly distressed, for the men spoke of stoning him
because the souls of them all were bitterly grieved, each man for his
sons and daughters...* (1 Samuel 30:6).

There would be a colossal turning point in this story. Would David
go down into the cavernous pit of outer darkness of the human soul?
Would he sink into isolation and depression and give up in the most
distressing, torturous moment of his life?

There is a point of *breaking* that we all face at some Ziklag experience. It might not be exactly like David's; your breaking point and mine
might not be the same. Yet, there is a time in every life when we realize

that we will either break or move our lives forward to maximize His glory—in spite of our crippling circumstances.

It was at this point of turning, that David made a decision that would be talked about to this day. What was that destiny decision? Very simply, David encouraged himself.

But David encouraged and strengthened himself in the Lord his God (1 Samuel 30:6).

How he did it, we are not told. I would like to think that David recalled the character and nature of God as he had done so poetically and prophetically since his days of isolation on the pastoral hillsides.

The Lord is my Light and my Salvation—whom shall I fear or dread? The Lord is the Refuge and Stronghold of my life—of whom shall I be afraid? (Psalm 27:1 AMP)

Maybe David thought about how many times God had spared his life up to that point.

Preserve me, O God: for in Thee do I put my trust (Psalm 16:1).

Or perhaps David simply praised God in the very place of indescribable emotional pain and injury.

I will love Thee, O Lord, my strength. The Lord is my rock, and my fortress, and my deliverer; my God, my strength, in whom I will trust; my buckler, and the horn of my salvation, and my high tower (Psalm 18:1-2).

Or maybe David went into immediate prayer, the womb of all hope.

For Thou art my hope, O Lord GOD: Thou art my trust from my youth (Psalm 71:5).

This move to encourage himself propelled enough fuel into David's empty "expectation tank" to move him into his next assignment.

And David said to Abiathar the priest, Ahimelech's son, I pray thee, bring me hither the ephod. And Abiathar brought thither the ephod to David. And David enquired at the Lord, saying, Shall I pursue after this troop? shall I overtake them? And He answered him, Pursue: for thou shalt surely overtake them, and without fail recover all (1 Samuel 30:7-8).

David asked God if he should go after the plunderers. God told David that he would win and that he would recover all. God is in the restoring business! Whatever it might be that you have lost or feel that you have lost, God has not lost anything. His inventory is still intact. His treasure house is still full. His client list still has your name on it. You are under His constant surveillance, and you have not dropped off God's radar screen.

Renew your expectation. Stir up your faith. Resurrect dead dreams. Your healing is on the way. Defeat, discouragement, and despair cannot stop you.

Live a life of expectation.

When Things Seem Out of Control

Sometimes, the jolts of life come one right after another. Just when you have cried out for recovery from one situation, another comes on its heels. In those moments, we wonder: "Does it ever end? How can I cope with one more deliberate strike?"

This is the time to know that God is our only refuge, and in Him alone, we can run the race.

God is our refuge and strength, a very present help in trouble (Psalm 46:1).

The time frame of 2001 to 2005 marked the most purging years of my life. I should be a statistic by now, and most people who knew me would have agreed—*but God can work in the middle of the most devastating crashes of life!* I saw a day that my faith was so shaken that everything that I thought I had ever believed was now in question. Had God failed me? Had He abandoned me at the worst possible moment? I thought He could not fail. Deep down, I knew that God had not failed and would never fail His people; but the perception of what seemed a discrepancy was very real in my mind.

Like Job, none of us can choose the timing of our fiery trials and relentless storms. Instead, we must learn the sustaining power of His grace. God is with us, even when we don't sense His nearness.

When thou passest through the waters, I will be with thee; and through the rivers, they shall not overflow thee: when thou walkest through the fire, thou shalt not be burned; neither shall the flame kindle upon thee (Isaiah 43:2).

Job was a man whose walk with God drew heavenly attention. Job was not perfect: He was not without sin or the flaws of humanity. Yet the Bible says Job was *"perfect."* In other words, Job pleased God. As far as he had come in life and as far as God was concerned, Job was perfect.

> *Job was a man who lived in Uz. He was honest inside and out, a man of his word, who was totally devoted to God and hated evil with a passion. He had seven sons and three daughters. He was also very wealthy—seven thousand head of sheep, three thousand camels, five hundred teams of oxen, five hundred donkeys, and a huge staff of servants—the most influential man in all the East!* (Job 1:1-3 MSG)

In spite of Job's devotion to God, and perhaps even because of it, his life became the object of attack.

Sometimes, the enemy tells us that the closer we get to God, the more bombardment is going to come our way. This deceptive enemy never tells us that the greater the conflict, the greater the victory. The word *victory* is not listed in his demonic dictionary. This lying spirit will never tell you that the more pressing the process, the greater the grace and glory of God can become upon your life.

Fear Came Upon Job.

For the thing which I greatly feared is come upon me, and that which I was afraid of is come unto me (Job 3:25).

Fear is a common cause of loss. Somehow, Job was never at peace and frequently thought, "What if I were to lose everything?" This thought, no doubt, persisted, until it finally manifested. Fear is a merciless robber. That's why we can never allow fear to become the fertile soil of demonic attack. It must be nipped in the bud. If not, the blessings of God can be lost.

Fear robs you of hope. Refuse fear. In its place, develop the confidence of God's love for you and His hopes for your life. Rest in the Lord. Allow good expectations to fill your thought process. Recall past victories. Study God's character. Stay in the Word. Stay in prayer.

There is a generation and a culture for you to reach. There are hurting individuals for whom God has assigned you to be a lifeline. It is only through the crushing of the olive that the oil is produced. Don't be amazed at the crushing of your hopes and dreams. Your process will work for you in the long run.

Job suffered the loss of his possessions, his cattle and animals that were used in sacrifice, his children, and his friends. Even his wife urged him to forsake God:

Then said his wife unto him, Dost thou still retain thine integrity? curse God, and die (Job 2:9).

Satan struck, and Job lost it all. What have you lost? Have you lost wealth, possessions, and friends? Have you buried loved one after loved one until you could no longer stand the dreadful pain of loss? Have your friends and loved ones abandoned you during a time of trial?

Like Job, this is not your time to die. Instead, this is the beginning of your finest hour. After the trials of Job, he lived another 140 years and enjoyed the perpetual blessings of the Lord upon his life.

After this lived Job an hundred and forty years, and saw his sons, and his sons' sons, even four generations (Job 42:16).

I am here to tell you that your season of trial is contained in a time frame. Your season of battle is coming to an end. You are getting ready for restoration.

And the Lord turned the captivity of Job, when he prayed for his friends: also the Lord gave Job twice as much as he had before (Job 42:10).

After Trial Comes Divine Promotion

The latter end of Job was more blessed than his beginning. Your latter will be greater than your past. You will enjoy your life so that you can be restored in total joy and peace, able to enjoy the blessings of God. In the end, you will see that your trials only served to promote you.

The tide will turn. We see that in Job's life. Satan saw the day that he would regret ever having touched God's "perfect" man. Even Job's friends who had mercilessly abandoned him came back to console him. Instead of bringing sorrow as they once did, they brought joy to God's man. Likewise in your life, some of the people who watched you fall are going to be there when you get up again. You have been set up for promotion! God has a "hope team" for your life.

_____

_____

_____

_____

_____

_____

_____

_____

_____

_____

_____

_____

_____

_____

_____

_____

_____

_____

_____

_____

_____

_____

_____

Hope
Journal

Hope Journal

CHAPTER SIX

This Is Not the Way to Live

Entrapment in the trial can become a captivating mind-set. You can exist in a state of repeated blows so long, you begin to believe that endless trials are normal, and life is supposed to be this way. You can begin to assume that each trial is a commercial for the next one. In order to cope, you mentally adjust to the foregone conclusion that your life will be one big trial with no hope for anything good. You seem doomed to the fate of a life of hurts, disappointments, and regrets.

It is at this point that unanswered prayers become magnified, and you accept the lie that God Himself is your enemy. Discouragement is up to the same old tricks again—satan loves to attack the integrity of your heavenly Father.

I recall the most excruciating time period of my life. *Before* that time, I *knew* that I had mountain-moving faith. I *knew* that I could conquer any difficulty. I *knew* that I could look insurmountable odds square in the face and come out victorious in Christ. *I knew* it! But then I faced the time in my life when my prayers didn't seem to work. The confessions of faith that I knew to speak only mocked me. The times of fasting only produced hunger. I anointed with oil, and nothing happened. Church services, where I left full of pain, only frustrated me more. I realize now, that without being fully aware of it, I had put too much faith in my own ability to have faith; I was not really resting in the grace of God to see me through the darkest storms of life.

I had to come to terms with an important spiritual principle:

For My thoughts are not your thoughts, neither are your ways My ways, saith the Lord. For as the heavens are higher than the earth, so are My ways higher than your ways, and My thoughts than your thoughts (Isaiah 55:8-9).

This is the time that I began to crawl back into the nursery of faith. Real faith. Not verbal confessions of faith, but the bedrock foundation of our faith.

Easton's 1897 Bible Dictionary states the following about faith:

Faith is in general the persuasion of the mind that a certain statement is true (see Phil. 1:27; 2 Thess. 2:13). Its primary idea is trust. A thing is true, and therefore worthy of trust. It admits of many degrees up to full assurance of faith, in accordance with the evidence on which it rests. Faith is the result of teaching (see Rom. 10:14-17). Knowledge is an essential element in all faith, and is sometimes spoken of as an equivalent to faith (see John 10:38; 1 John 2:3). Yet the two are distinguished in this respect, that faith includes in it assent, which is an act of the will in addition to the act of the understanding. Assent to the truth is of the essence of faith, and the ultimate ground on which our assent to any revealed truth rests is the veracity of God. Historical faith is the apprehension of and assent to certain statements which are regarded as mere facts of history. Temporary faith is that state of mind which is awakened in men (e.g., Felix) by the exhibition of the truth and by the influence of religious sympathy, or by what is sometimes styled the common operation of the Holy Spirit. Saving faith is so called because it has eternal life inseparably connected with it. It cannot be better defined than in the words of the Assembly's Shorter Catechism: "Faith in Jesus Christ is a saving grace, whereby we receive and rest upon him alone for salvation, as he is offered to us in the gospel." The object of saving faith is the whole revealed Word of God. Faith accepts and believes it as the very truth most sure. But the special act of faith which unites to Christ has as its object the person and the work of the Lord Jesus Christ (see John 7:38; Acts 16:31). This is the specific act of faith by which a sinner is justified before God (see Rom. 3:22, 25; Gal. 2:16; Phil. 3:9; John 3:16-36; Acts 10:43; 16:31). In this act of faith the believer appropriates and rests on Christ alone as Mediator in all his offices. This assent to or belief in the truth received upon the divine testimony has always associated with it a deep sense of sin, a distinct view of Christ, a consenting will, and a loving heart, together with a reliance on, a trusting in, or resting in Christ. It is that state of mind in which a poor sinner, conscious of his sin, flees from his guilty self to Christ his Saviour, and rolls over the burden of all his sins on him. It consists chiefly, not in the assent given to the testimony of God in his Word, but in embracing with fiducial reliance and trust the one and only Saviour whom God reveals. This trust and reliance is of the essence of faith. By faith the believer directly and immediately appropriates Christ as his own. Faith in its direct act makes Christ ours. It is not a work which God graciously accepts instead of perfect obedience, but is only the hand by which we take hold of the person and work of our Redeemer as the only ground of our salvation. Saving faith is a moral act, as it proceeds from a renewed will, and a renewed will is necessary to believing assent to the truth of God (see 1 Cor. 2:14; 2 Cor. 4:4). Faith, therefore, has its seat in the moral part of our nature fully as much as in the intellectual. The mind must first be enlightened by divine teaching (see John 6:44; Acts 13:48; 2 Cor. 4:6; Eph. 1:17,18) before it can discern the things of the Spirit. Faith is necessary to our salvation (see Mark 16:16), not because there is any merit in it, but simply because it is the sinner's taking the place assigned him by God, his falling in with what God is doing. The warrant or ground of faith is the divine testimony, not the reasonableness of what God says, but the simple fact that he says it. Faith rests immediately on "Thus saith the Lord." But in order to this faith the veracity, sincerity, and truth of God must be owned and appreciated, together with his unchangeableness. God's word encourages and emboldens the sinner personally to transact with Christ as God's gift, to close with him, embrace him, give himself to Christ, and take Christ as his. That word comes with power, for it is the word of God who has revealed himself in his works, and especially in the cross. God is to be believed for his word's sake, but also for his name's sake. Faith in Christ secures for the believer freedom from condemnation, or justification before God; a participation in the life that is in Christ, the divine life (see John 14:19; Rom. 6:4-10; Eph. 4:15,16, etc.); "peace with God" (see Rom. 5:1); and sanctification (see Acts 26:18; Gal. 5:6; Acts 15:9). All who thus believe in Christ will certainly be saved (see John 6:37, 40; 10:27, 28; Rom. 8:1). The faith = the Gospel (see Acts 6:7; Rom. 1:5; Gal. 1:23; 1 Tim. 3:9; Jude 1:3).[1]

I took a journey back into the most basic belief on which all of Christianity stands. I left my acquired knowledge of faith and its daily operation in the life of the believer. I stopped relying on the plentiful experiences of faith in what God had done for me in the past. I no longer appealed to my sense of the faith formulas upon which I had previously leaned. These were all well and good, but I was in a desperate situation and had to find the bedrock of my belief. I was being stripped away, layer by layer, and somewhere under all of this, I had to find the Rock that would not move. If my foundation rested on formulas or past successes, my foundation would continue to fail me. But if I could plant my life upon something far greater than my learned abilities in faith, then perhaps I would be able to emerge from this season with an unfailing faith in an unfailing Savior.

That is exactly what happened. I think this is most likely what Jesus meant when He told Peter that He had prayed for the effectiveness of Peter's faith:

> But I have prayed for thee, **that thy faith fail not:** and when thou art converted, strengthen thy brethren (Luke 22:32).

I like it even better in *The Message Bible*:

Simon, stay on your toes. Satan has tried his best to separate all of you from Me, like chaff from wheat. Simon, I've prayed for you in particular that you not give in or give out. When you have come through the time of testing, turn to your companions and give them a fresh start (Luke 22:31-32 MSG).

Once I understood that the strength of my position was always in Christ, my confidence skyrocketed. The strength of my position is always in Christ. We fail. People fail. Formulas fail. They are not what Jesus died to give us; what He died for was our "*in Christ*" position!

The sacrifice of Christ began to come into clearer focus. His grace, His life, His death, His Resurrection were all gifts to me and to my life. No trial will ever change that. No moments or lifetimes of adversity could ever change what He did for me. I went back to that.

You can, too! Begin to see yourself right now in your "in Christ" position. None of us deserves it; is not based on our faith formulas, or our perspectives on adversity. Being in Christ is a "gift" position. We are here by grace and not by our own gifts. This place is His gift to us, not our gift to Him.

If my gift had gotten me here, I would be lost now, because even my gifts failed me. But since I am here by the gift of God, I now have a solid foundation on which to build.

The strength of my position is always in Christ. Right now, repeat that statement over and over until you begin to know that your strength is in your "in Christ" position, and no storm can ever change that!

Remember this: He chose you to be His and arranged for His righteousness to be yours.

According as He hath chosen us in Him before the foundation of the world, that we should be holy and without blame before Him in love... (Ephesians 1:4).

And be found in Him, not having mine own righteousness, which is of the law, but that which is through the faith of Christ, the righteousness which is of God by faith... (Philippians 3:9).

The Thief and the Robber

When hope is carved out of our lives by the sharp blades of calamity, our enemy begins to work at destroying our access to God's ability. Satan, like religion, is not just a thief, but a robber.

Verily, verily, I say unto you, He that entereth not by the door into the sheepfold, but climbeth up some other way, the same is a thief and a robber (John 10:1).

You see if he were only a thief, the torture would not be quite as severe. But he is also a robber.

A thief takes the goods or property of another by stealth without the victim's knowledge: like a thief in the night. A robber trespasses upon the house, property, or person of another, and makes away with things of value, even at the cost of violence.

This is the work of satan. He not only steals, but he threatens, he trespasses, and he uses force and violence. Cruelty is his specialty.

Webster's dictionary defines the word *threaten* as "an expression of intention to inflict evil, injury, or damage; one that threatens; an indication of something impending."[2]

When the enemy strikes with his robbery and intimidation, he will threaten you, telling you that all your hopes are lost forever and that you can never recover or rebuild from loss and brokenness. He will tell you that it is impossible to recover from the agonizing situations of life.

This is much worse than a thief—this is robbery. He is attempting to hold you hostage. Recognize the enemy. He is not out to pat you on the back when you have been devastated. Instead, he opportunistically moves in with his weapons to mock the Word of God over your life. The battle right now is over the integrity of the Word of God in your life. It's time to take a stand to enforce the victory that Jesus has already obtained for everyone who will believe. The destiny-robber has been exposed!

Mark chapter 4 gives us the parable of the sower and the seed. Over and over again, the emphasis is upon the seed. The seed gets planted, the seed overcomes, the seed grows, the seed multiplies. The seed, the seed, the seed.

The seeds of life, the seeds of hope, the seeds of promise, the seeds of potential, the seeds of destiny have all been planted into the believer at the new birth. This is the Word of God that has been sown into your heart when you became a Christian. Satan always comes to steal the Word that has been sown into our lives.

And these are they by the way side, where the word is sown; but when they have heard, Satan cometh immediately, and taketh away the word that was sown in their hearts (Mark 4:15).

Satan hates the Word and will use every weapon within his arsenal to destroy our perception of God's integral Word working powerfully in our lives.

God's Word is self-sufficient. In other words, standing alone, it has procreative power. That's why the first thing satan does is to target the integrity of God's Word. Satan's mission is to prove the Word to be unsuccessful in our lives.

However, God's Word is settled. When everything else is shaken, God's Word still stands.

For the Word that God speaks is alive and full of power [making it active, operative, energizing, and effective]; it is sharper than any two-edged sword, penetrating to the dividing line of the breath of life (soul) and [the immortal] spirit, and of joints and marrow [of the deepest parts of our nature], exposing and sifting and analyzing and judging the very thoughts and purposes of the heart (Hebrews 4:12 AMP).

Get Back Into the Word

If you can understand at this critical time in your life that the real battle being fought is over the integrity of God's Word, you will be empowered to refute the enemy and prevail over him. God's Word has the power and ability to work in you, even when you feel that all hope is lost. It is not time to quit. It is not time to give up on the Word of God.

In the thick of my sorrow, I can remember being curled up on the floor with my CD player. All I could do was to press the *play* button and listen. I was in the roughest of seas, and no life preservers were being thrown in my direction. I had to assimilate God's Word of hope into my being somehow.

Over and over, I would hear His promises spoken. I was devastated, thrown overboard, and taking in water. I had no choice but to keep the Word of God continually feeding into my spirit. I understand that we experience waves of trials that crash upon us to muffle the voice of God's Word in our lives. I also know that is the time to forge ahead. Don't forget God's Word, even when sadness is all-consuming and life is unbearable.

I will delight myself in Your statutes; I will not forget Your word (Psalm 119:16 AMP).

This is the very moment that you need the Word of God to be your refuge.

Every word of God is tried and purified; He is a shield to those who trust and take refuge in Him (Proverbs 30:5 AMP).

The breath of God will speak life to your decaying situation. At this moment, it is possible that the only breath you have is that which comes forth from the Word of God. That is because Scripture comes directly from the "breath" of God.

Every Scripture is God-breathed (given by His inspiration) and profitable for instruction, for reproof and conviction of sin, for correction of error and discipline in obedience, [and] for training in righteousness (in holy living, in conformity to God's will in thought, purpose, and action) (2 Timothy 3:16 AMP).

Don't Suffocate During Your Battle

God's Word will produce an effect in your life. It is no wonder that this is one of the first areas that satan seeks to erode. When satan is attacking the Word in your life, it is because of the potency of the seed. God's Word is a powerful force.

> *So shall My word be that goes forth out of My mouth: it shall not return to Me void [without producing any effect, useless], but it shall accomplish that which I please and purpose, and it shall prosper in the thing for which I sent it* (Isaiah 55:11 AMP).

When the serpent came to captivate and deceive in The Garden of Eden, he had a technique. The enemy has not changed his schemes or cunning devices. There is a system to this battle. There is a strategy at work. If you know the line of attack, you are authorized to go in and intercept and prevent further injury from the enemy. One of the enemy's first modes of operation is to cast doubt on the Word, just as he did with Eve. Satan disguises himself. He subtly and slyly shifts our focus away from God. He attacks God's Word.

He attacks God's character and His ability to be good to His children.

Watch how he casts doubt on the Word of God:

> *Now the serpent was more subtle than any beast of the field which the Lord God had made. And he said unto the woman, Yea, hath God said, Ye shall not eat of every tree of the garden?* (Genesis 3:1)

The serpent was the shrewdest of all the wild animals the Lord God had made. One day he asked the woman, "Did God really say you must not eat the fruit from any of the trees in the garden?" (Genesis 3:1 NLT)

Did God *really* say? Did God really say that He loved you? Did God really say that He was going to deliver you? Did God really say that He answers prayer? Really? Are you sure? Absolutely sure? Did God really mean what He said? This is his ploy. He knows he is powerless in the face of God's compelling, effective Word. So, he ever casts suspicion on the veracity of that Word.

I remember crying out to God in the dark of my isolation: "Is this how it feels to die of a broken heart? Because I don't think I'm going to make it through this night." I hurt all over, inside and out. My chest was heavy; my breathing was labored; my heart was in fragile shards.

Thoughts were running marathons inside of my being. Every word God had ever given me was being tried. What I didn't know at the time was that God was going to use my battle to prepare a turning point for someone else.

God will use your battle as a turning point.

Your emotional erosion or ongoing emotional health will always be attached to your thinking. Your thinking, as a believer, is in direct connection to the Word of God that is active in your life. If your thoughts are focused on the Word, your emotions and life will reflect that.

Finally, brethren, whatsoever things are true, whatsoever things are honest, whatsoever things are just, whatsoever things are pure, whatsoever things are lovely, whatsoever things are of good report; if there be any virtue, and if there be any praise, think on these things (Philippians 4:8).

The Word of God determines the way you think. The way you think determines the way you feel. The way you feel determines the decisions you make. The decisions you make determine the way you act. The way you act determines the habits you form in life. Your habits in life become your character. Your character will shape you for your destiny.

Satan knows that your thinking is the only way that he can set up a stronghold, which is a demonic fortification established by wrong thinking. That is his method to destroy your life and annihilate your purpose.

This is why his first line of attack is against the integrity of God's nature, character, and Word. The enemy knows that cumulative trials have a way of chipping away our tender hopes in God. When our hope is gone, faith has nothing to stick to.

Your situation is not hopeless. There are really no hopeless situations, only people who feel hopeless in their situations. It might seem hopeless to you, but not to God. Years ago, while I was walking through a deep, deep pit, I said to my husband, "Bill, I feel like I am not going to make it through this." He wisely and lovingly said to me, "You may not *feel* like you will, but you really do *know* you will, don't you?"

To be perfectly honest, there are a lot of times that I don't know the way to take out of the maze of life. I haven't seen the map. But I know the Map-Maker, and I am called to trust Him.

There are some things you might not *feel,* but because you know God, you *know* He is going to see you through your situation. You have not come through whatever you have been through to give up now. Don't throw in the towel. Your story is not over. God is going to make this test a testimony. He is going to make this mess a message. He is going to make this trial a blessing, and He is going to restore your hope.

Endnotes

1. Faith. Dictionary.com. Easton's 1897 Bible Dictionary, http://dictionary.reference.com/browse/faith (accessed: December 17, 2009).

2. Merriam-Webster Online Dictionary. 2009, s.v. "threaten," http://www.merriam-webster.com/dictionary/threaten (accessed December 21, 2009).

Hope
Journal

Hope
Journal

CHAPTER SEVEN

Turning Hopeless Situations Around

Hopeless situations can be turned around. All things are still possible for the person who will take a stand in the Word of God. With God, there is always hope.

Moses, the man of God, took matters into his own hands and killed an Egyptian who struck a Hebrew man (see Exod. 2:11). As a result, Moses fled to Midian to escape Pharaoh's wrath. It would be 40 years before Moses would return to Egypt and his ministry to the Israelites.

Still, God's hand never left Moses, in spite of the fact that he murdered someone. You might have some regrets in your life, but God is calling others to come alongside and help to turn you back toward your destiny and out of the land of Midian. You will not be robbed any longer! Enough of these destiny-robbers!

You might be in the trenches dug by painful tragedies right now. Your story might not be airing on the evening news or blogged about on the

Internet—yet the circumstances cause you to question God's plan and ask, "Why?" Remember that whenever He allows you to question Him, He is giving you an opportunity to share His hope in a new dimension.

Eric Clapton, possibly the greatest living rock guitarist, wrote a heartrending song about the death of his four-year-old son, Conor, on March 20, 1991, after the boy fell from a 53rd-story window in New York City.[1]

Clapton took nine months off, and when he returned, his music had changed. The hardship had a tremendous effect; Clapton's music became softer, more powerful, and more reflective. He wrote a song titled "Tears in Heaven" about his son's death. It is an emotional ballad, filled with hope. Even so our hearts ached when five of our family members went through an unseen heavenly door. But we have God's irrevocable promise that He, Himself, will wipe away every tear from our eyes. We have a hope.

> *And God shall wipe away all tears from their eyes; and there shall be no more death, neither sorrow, nor crying, neither shall there be any more pain* (Revelation 21:4).

Jesus told us how to deal with emotional pain. He said: *"Do not let your hearts be troubled. Trust in God; trust also in Me"* (John 14:1 NIV).

I understand the pain we experience when we lose a loved one. After Hayley's burial, the 90-minute drive from the cemetery to our house was filled with pain and reflection. It all seemed so senseless. We had questions. Hayley was only 20 years old. As a blended family, we'd had our share of ups and downs. It seemed that the last couple of years before the accident were especially challenging. However, powerful moments in prayer had softened and tenderized our individual perspectives, leaving us with optimistic anticipation.

Still, tragedy struck. "Dad, Hayley won't get to be with us for Thanksgiving," Jordan cried just days before our holiday meal.

Bill glanced over his shoulder to look at our eight-year-old son. Jordan was filled with hurt and confusion about his sister's death. Bill responded to Jordan's suffering, saying, "Yes she will, son. She will always be with us. She's in our heart, and she will always be in our heart." I had seen this kind of reinforced, gentle strength in my husband many times before, but this time, there was supernatural trust in the most difficult of heartbreaks. I could hear it in his voice. Later on, I would use very similar words to let our son know that, like Hayley, Boodle, Papa Corn, Papa Deerman, and now Dad, too, would always be in our heart.

We are always called to trust God. Experiences might disorient us with bitterness and pain, but our trust assures us that God is eager to restore us to unmoved hope in Him.

We each need to put our trust in God to build strength to stand against the battles ahead. The way to do this is to get back to the basics. Don't try to be overly deep, especially in the midst of trials. Just be basic in your approach. God will honor your simple steps of faith.

There is no situation in your life too difficult for God to turn around. You never have to overcome God's reluctance; you just simply have to know how to lay hold of His willingness. He will give you everything you need to place your trust in Him if you will show Him that you are willing.

God has a tomorrow for you. He has a plan for you.

Jesus Christ [is] *the same yesterday, and to day, and for ever* (Hebrews 13:8).

Jesus has already been in your yesterdays; He is in your todays; and He has already walked through your tomorrows. You are going to make it. He has already been there.

I like the story about the boy and his father who were planning a fishing trip. The evening before, as the father put his son to bed, the boy hugged his father's neck and said, *"Daddy, thank you for tomorrow."*

Now is the time to thank your heavenly Father for the faith for today and the hope for tomorrow. God has new opportunities for you. He has surprising adventures planned! Hitch up with God and let Him plow with you through the fields of your future. He will help you through the sharp rocks of adversity, the boulders of disappointments, and the hard places of life. He will teach you how to plant the seeds for your future harvest. And He will give you enough of the sweet nectar of life to make the bitter places palatable.

"Now" Hope Equals Future Faith

A little over a month before he died, the famous atheist Jean-Paul Sartre declared that he so strongly resisted feelings of despair that he would say to himself, "I know I shall die in hope." Then in profound sadness, he would add, "But hope needs a foundation."[2]

I am here to tell you that hope's foundation is the Word of God. Hope will produce a life-giving effect.

A number of years ago, researchers performed an experiment to see the effect hope has on those undergoing hardship. Two sets of laboratory rats were placed in separate tubs of water. The researchers left one set in the water and found that within an hour, they all drowned. The other rats were periodically lifted out of the water and then returned. As a result, the second set of rats continued to swim for more than 24 hours.

Why? Not because they were given a rest, but because they were given hope! Those animals somehow hoped that if they could stay afloat just a little longer, someone would reach down and rescue them. If hope holds such power for unthinking rodents, how much greater should its effect be on our lives.

Hezekiah, a king in the Old Testament, was in what appeared to be a hopeless situation. King Hezekiah was not a perfect man, but he had a heart that was turned toward God.

> *In those days was Hezekiah sick unto death. And Isaiah the prophet the son of Amoz came unto him, and said unto him, Thus saith the Lord, Set thine house in order: for thou shalt die, and not live. Then Hezekiah turned his face toward the wall, and prayed unto the Lord, and said, Remember now, O Lord, I beseech Thee, how I have walked before Thee in truth and with a perfect heart, and have done that which is good in Thy sight. And Hezekiah wept sore. Then came the word of the Lord to Isaiah, saying, Go, and say to Hezekiah, Thus saith the Lord, the God of David thy father, I have heard thy prayer, I have seen thy tears: behold, I will add unto thy days fifteen years* (Isaiah 38:1-5).

Hezekiah had been given a death sentence. But just when his situation looked hopeless, he turned his face toward the wall and started seeking God. To turn your face toward the wall simply means that you turn away from everything else that is pulling you, distracting you, or taking your focus away from God and His plans for you.

This is what King Hezekiah did. He looked away from every distraction until all he could see was God. Have you ever shot a gun at a target? Usually, you take your time and you just focus and stare—and you continue to stare at the target until all you see is the target.

Sometimes, things happen in our lives, and we are forced into a place where nothing but God gets our attention. Hezekiah even turned from the prophet Isaiah in order to fully seek the face of God.

Your experiences have brought you here. Now, go before God and God alone, and tell Him the thoughts of your heart. He knows them anyway. Let Him hear your voice, as Hezekiah did. Show God your tears. Hezekiah showed God his tears. He fully revealed his heart to the Lord.

Sometimes, we have to get into emergency mode. There is no time for games or for chance. We go in before God to live or else we stay where we are and die. We must become willing to lay aside every distraction.

Draw the Life-and-Death Line

"Are you all right, Jana?" our missions director yelled from the shore of a Central American island.

Worriedly, I screamed out through the roar of the waves, "Yeah." In actuality, I had only seconds to stay up.

Our team of young college-student missionaries had only been on the island for two days. It was total paradise—a little land mass a half-mile wide and three miles long, right in the middle of the azure Caribbean Sea.

Surrounded by thatch huts and huge iguanas, we went spear-fishing for our meals and ate lobsters as soon as they were caught. It was paradise. Little did I know that I was about to have a near-death experience that I would never forget.

The island had been split in two by a hurricane sometime in the 1960s. This caused a channel known as *The Split*. It was at least 25 feet deep and wide enough for ships to pass through. It also created a raging current that led straight to open sea.

One afternoon, all of us decided to go snorkeling at The Split. While in shallow water, I saw the most beautiful, colorful shell I had ever seen, floating on top of the sea. I reached to grab the "shell"; when I did, I heard one of the missionaries scream. "Don't touch it, Jana! It's a man of war!"

I panicked and took off my face mask. Holding the mask tightly, I swam frantically. I saw a clump of trees to my left and began to swim around them. When I turned the corner, I got caught up in the middle of the channel. I have never been a confident swimmer, but I had no choice; I had to go for it. I was way over my head and things didn't look good. I became separated from all of the other snorkelers. Fear paralyzed me. I was afraid that I wasn't going to make it.

Things were about to get worse. Much worse.

With panic setting in and disabling my ability to think straight, I began to fight the current, swimming with the face mask still in my hand. Why didn't I just drop it? Why didn't I let it go? With each stroke, I was fighting to pull up what felt like a bucket of water.

"I'll just go down and try to touch bottom. This channel may not be that deep," I reasoned. Not finding any bottom, I summoned the strength to get back to the top for another breath and push for my life. By this time, I could see about 20 of our group on the shore. All of them were oblivious to the seriousness of the waves that threatened me. The currents were raging and swiftly taking me out to open sea.

"Please help me, Jesus," I begged for my life. I decided to go down again and try to find bottom. Again, there was no place for my feet. With all the strength I could muster, I surfaced for another breath and fought some more.

With my face mask still in hand, I tried to swim across the current to the shore. I had so far to go; the channel was so deep. I was so tired. I had no more energy. I focused on trying one more time. Maybe I could touch bottom and push off for a little more hope. For the final time, I went down in the unruly waters.

A surreal peace invaded my soul as I quickly examined my life. "God, do I have peace with You? If I don't make it, am I prepared to meet You?"

I don't know how, but I came back up and began to push against the current and make my way toward the bank. By this time, the face mask had become a fixture in my hand. I don't know why I refused to let the thing go. It sure wasn't valuable. Looking back, maybe it had become my security blanket. Nevertheless, I was in a furious current in 25 feet of water. I was heading out to open sea without a life preserver. The face mask had become a life-threatening distraction.

That's when I heard our director yell, "Are you all right, Jana?" If I said I wasn't all right, others would surely drown along with me. How sad and useless that would have been. Instead, God was going to reveal His hand and let me know that He had a future and a hope for my life!

The next time I looked toward land, all the missionaries had formed a human chain out to open sea, anchoring themselves by the roots of a tree on the bank.

Inspired by help, at that moment, I loosed that cheap little face mask from my hand and pushed with all of my strength and the strength of the Lord toward my human hope-rope, anchored by the roots of the tree.

Collapsing into the arms of caring people never felt so good! I was back on land, saved from death. It was clear that the fight was so much more difficult because I would not let go of my face mask. What I was holding on to almost cost me my life.

What are you holding on to that needs to be released? What kinds of distractions have become that important to you? I might as well say it: What kind of "face-mask" are you holding on to right now? Let it go. It's not worth it.

Looking away [from all that will distract] to Jesus, Who is the Leader and the Source of our faith [giving the first incentive for our belief] and is also its Finisher [bringing it to maturity and perfection]. He, for the joy [of obtaining the prize] that was set before Him, endured the cross, despising and ignoring the shame, and is now seated at the right hand of the throne of God (Hebrews 12:2 AMP).

God's plans for you are far better than you could ever dream. God doesn't see things as men see them. God looks on the heart.

...for the Lord seeth not as man seeth; for man looketh on the outward appearance, but the Lord looketh on the heart (1 Samuel 16:7).

Even when you have failed, missed the mark, or sinned, God still looks at your heart and intentions. God is not holding your sins against you. After repentance, God forgets about your sins.

He will turn again, He will have compassion upon us; He will subdue our iniquities; and Thou wilt cast all their sins into the depths of the sea (Micah 7:19).

Some of you need to hang a "no fishing" sign out. Don't bring up something God has chosen to forget. Repentance changes everything. When others are involved, seek the redeeming grace of God. God's heart is always reconciliation wherever it is possible. There will always be people who reject your attempts at reconciliation and restitution. You are not responsible for someone else's response to God's Word. God loves all of humanity, and He has such a way of redeeming people through the most difficult of circumstances. God is love, and He will deal with each of us on an individual basis.

So then every one of us shall give account of himself to God (Romans 14:12).

Don't allow your past to stop you from moving into your future. Your life is not about your past—it is about the now moments and the now moments yet to be created. Your past cannot stop God from turning a hopeless perspective around.

Remember that others are loved by God, too. Don't judge others because of their situation. It is not up to you to settle the ultimate sovereignty of God over your life or over anyone else's.

Don't pick on people, jump on their failures, criticize their faults—unless, of course, you want the same treatment. That critical spirit has a way of boomeranging. It's easy to see a smudge on your neighbor's face and be oblivious to the ugly sneer on your own. Do you have the nerve to say, "Let me wash your face for you," when your own face is distorted by contempt? It's this whole traveling road-show mentality all over again, playing a holier-than-thou part instead of just living your part. Wipe that ugly sneer off your own face, and you might be fit to offer a washcloth to your neighbor (Matthew 7:1-5 MSG).

How many times along the road of life have you come to a dead-end situation? This is the time to renew your trust in God. He loves you, and He cares.

We don't want you in the dark, friends, about how hard it was when all this came down on us in Asia province. It was so bad we didn't think we were going to make it. We felt like we'd been sent to death row, that it was all over for us. As it turned out, it was the best thing that could have happened. Instead of trusting in our own strength or wits to get out of it, we were forced to trust God totally—not a bad idea since He's the God who raises the dead! And He did it, rescued us from certain doom. And He'll do it again, rescuing us as many times as we need rescuing. You and your prayers are part of the rescue operation—I don't want you in the dark about that either. I can see your faces even now, lifted in praise for God's deliverance of us, a rescue in which your prayers played such a crucial part (2 Corinthians 1:8-11 MSG).

Paul did not see a hopeless situation as an ultimate dead end. He looked at it from a hopeful perspective. Endings are a time of new beginnings. Maybe some things in your life are on the permanent wrap-up; maybe some things are just over with for good. You can take this opportunity to watch God forge a new beginning for you, and He will. Yes, it might be the end—the end of what you are going through. Maybe you need to say aloud right now: "This is the end of what I have been going through. God has a new beginning for me now."

Build your confidence for your new beginning. Don't let self-doubt rob you. Refuse to be undermined by belittling thoughts about yourself. Don't let anyone else's opinion of you form your reality. Stabilization will return to your life as you begin to build your confidence of who you are in Christ Jesus. Your self-worth, self-esteem, and self-value already have been determined in Christ Jesus. This has not changed. Get back to this basic building block of life.

Gideon, in the Old Testament, was a man who had a very poor opinion of himself. He was filled with doubt and fear. Cowardice overwhelmed him. But the Angel of the Lord came to Gideon and called him a name he would never have called himself.

And the angel of the Lord appeared unto him, and said unto him, The Lord is with thee, thou mighty man of valour (Judges 6:12).

You might see yourself one way, but God sees you another. Don't set your opinions in stone until you consult God's opinions. His are the ones that carry the real weight. The deciding factor comes when you cast your vote. Will you agree with God? He never gives up on you. He has already decided what is best for your life, and He knows that you are more than able to walk in His best.

Ask God to reveal your immeasurable value. Ask Him for strength to walk in His Word and in His estimation of your life. He is the One who stands ready to help you begin again. He is ready to give you a new start, to wipe away your tears, and to take you by the hand into your new future. You can make another attempt at life, regardless of the pains you have suffered. Pursue the goals that God has placed before you. You are 100 percent safe in the hands of a caring, confident, all-knowing God.

With confidence, start out in the race knowing that you have already won. Take action. Don't sit on the sidelines with self-doubt growing like fungi in a science lab. Move forward. Baby steps are better than no steps at all! The journey of a thousand miles begins with one step. Take it today.

Quit judging yourself through other people's eyes, or even through your own. Trials might have fogged your perspectives right now. Wipe off your lenses and readjust. Replace those irritating, scratchy lenses with some new ones. He wants to clear your vision. Always look through the lens of the Word of God and the vision of the Holy Spirit for your life.

God is with you whether you feel like it or not. You have to stay fixed on God and fixed on what God says about you—not what you feel and not what you perceive.

Difficult things have happened to most people on various levels of life. Troubles have come to us all. The turbulent wind that has hit you is not where your focus needs to be. Rather, your focus should be in the direction of your sail. There is time to turn your life around!

Man that is born of a woman is of few days and full of trouble (Job 14:1).

Tough things happen in life. Sometimes, life writes you a check, and you have to go out and cover it. Start building your confidence now. The sooner you do so, the better. You can get out of life's basement, even if you have to dig your way out with your own hands. The Holy Spirit is your Helper.

I know you have been stunned. I know you have been confused. I know you have been through a season of "shock and awe." However, God is not through with you. Your story is not over. You can hope again.

Take the old prophets as your mentors. They put up with anything, went through everything, and never once quit, all the time honoring God. What a gift life is to those who stay the course! You've heard, of course, of Job's staying power, and you know how God brought it all together for him at the end. That's because God cares, cares right down to the last detail (James 5:10-11 MSG).

In taking the time to rebuild your confidence, you will have many opportunities to be stretched in the area of endurance. You are not a quitter. You are going to elevate your endurance level, and you are going to finish the race that God has for you.

You can boost your endurance level by following four steps:

1. *Surround yourself with encouraging believers.* Search for caring hearts that know about the faithfulness of God. It's time to be encouraged about God's hopes for your life now. Focus on encouragement. Stay away from skeptics and those who do not celebrate your life. Stay away from religious clichés that hold no answers. The atmosphere of encouragement will feed new hopes for your life.

2. *Lay aside every weight that you should not be carrying.* Don't try to be a hero. Quit trying to live up to everybody else's expectations. Don't be a savior. We are responsible to people, not "for" people. You don't have to carry the weight of the world on your shoulders.

3. *Don't dwell on the past.* Not one of us can change five minutes ago. The windshield of life is bigger than the rearview mirror! Release and let go! Look ahead! God has promised to do a new thing! The Word of God shouts with hope for our futures!

    Remember not the former things (Isaiah 43:18).

    It's time to move forward, not backward. This is a Christian race. No runner races while looking backward! The direction is forward! Move on!

4. *Setting your eyes on Jesus.* Jesus had amazing endurance. He kept on in the face of every adversity. Stay focused. You will make it only if you keep your eyes on the Lord Jesus.

Young William Wilberforce was discouraged one night in the early 1790s after another defeat in his 10-year battle against the slave trade in England. Tired and frustrated, he opened his Bible and began to leaf through it. A small piece of paper fell out and fluttered to the floor. It was a letter written by John Wesley shortly before his death.[3] Wilberforce read it again:

> Unless the divine power has raised you up...I see not how you can go through your glorious enterprise in opposing that... [abominable practice of slavery] which is the scandal of religion, of England, and of human nature. Unless God has raised you up for this very thing, you will be worn out by the opposition of men and devils. But if God be for you, who can be against you? Are all of them together stronger than God? Oh, be not weary of well-doing. Go on in the name of God, and in the power of His might.[4]

Zig Ziglar, the celebrated motivational speaker, says, "You cannot consistently perform in a manner which is inconsistent with the way you see yourself."[5]

More Than a Conqueror

Recently while in Johannesburg, South Africa, I heard firsthand of the love and respect of the Africans for world leader Dr. Nelson Mandela. He spent 27 years in prison before he became president of South Africa. He made this remarkable quote, "The greatest glory in living lies not in never falling, but in rising every time we fall."[6]

Famed chemist Louis Pasteur said of himself, "Let me tell you the secret that has led me to my goal: My strength lies solely in my tenacity."[7]

Be tenacious! The dictionary definition for *tenacious* is "not easily pulled apart."[8] People with tenacity are not easily derailed by difficulty.

What has tried to tear you apart? What has happened in your life that has tempted you to believe that God was no longer for you?

I've got the greatest press release in the universe: God is for you!

What shall we then say to these things? If God be for us, who can be against us? (Romans 8:31)

Your breakthrough must come. Never doubt who God is. Never doubt who you are. Never doubt your ability to be productive in Christ. You are called. You are anointed. You have a God-given dream. Your destiny is bigger than you can ever know.

Open your mouth and speak the Word of God over your life.

Endnotes

1. "Eric Clapton's Son Killed in a 49-Story Fall" *New York Times*, March 21, 1991, http://www.nytimes.com/1991/03/21/nyregion/eric-clapton-s-son-killed-in-a-49-story-fall.html?pagewanted=1 (accessed December 21, 2009).

2. http://net.bible.org/illustration.php?id=1437.

3. Source: http://www.wesleyfamily.net/John.htm.

4. Source: http://www.wesleyfamily.net/John.htm.

5. Source: http://tomziglar.com/2009/03/13/thank-you-zig-ziglar-2/.

6. "African Success: Biography of Nelson MANDELA." *African Success: People Changing the Face of Africa*, http://www.africansuccess.org/.

7. "Louis Pasteur Quotes." *Famous Quotes and Authors, Famous Quotations for all Occasions*, http://www.famousquotesandauthors.com/authors/louis_pasteur_quotes.html.

8. Merriam-Webster Online Dictionary. 2009, s.v. "tenacious," http://www.merriam-webster.com/dictionary/tenacious (accessed December 21, 2009).

_____

_____

_____

_____

_____

_____

_____

_____

_____

_____

_____

_____

_____

_____

_____

_____

_____

_____

_____

_____

_____

_____

_____

_____

_____

Hope
Journal

Hope
Journal

CHAPTER EIGHT

Lost Hope Restored

The Day Paul Lost All Hope

The Bible is full of real-life stories of people, perhaps just like you, whose hopes and dreams were dashed to the ground.

You read about one of these people in Chapter 3 of this book. It was the apostle Paul who, at the time, was a prisoner on his way to Rome. While he and others were on board the ship, a storm arose. This was no ordinary storm. It was not a slight wind with a few boisterous waves. This was the wind that no sailor ever wanted to experience. There could be death in this wind, and there certainly would be damage.

At one point, the ship had to be lightened. Therefore, goods and provisions were thrown overboard. The storm was brutal, yet Paul's work was not yet done.

Sometimes, in order to take us higher in our journey, certain things have to shift in our lives. We have to leave the concerns that we don't understand, recognize, know, and comprehend in the hands of the Lord. At times, our ship of life has to be lightened. Maybe there are things we thought we could never live without or do without. Then, suddenly, we find ourselves in a place where these places or things or even people are somehow gone from our lives.

We have to remember that nothing in our lives is really ours. Even our loved ones are lent to us from the Lord. Sometimes, you might think "What if the worst thing happened to me?" For some of us, the worst possible outcome has already occurred. Yet, for whatever reason, we are still here. The letting go of what we think we need in life, what we think we deserve, what we believe we should be able to lay claim to, is all a part of our surrender to our God, who alone is able to make all grace abound in spite of the situation.

> *And God is able to make all grace (every favor and earthly blessing) come to you in abundance, so that you may always and under all circumstances and whatever the need be self-sufficient...* (2 Corinthians 9:8 AMP).

We are stewards, not owners, of what God allows us to have. A steward is one who watches over things that belong to someone else. We are stewards, not owners. God is the Master, Owner, and Possessor of all things.

> *The earth is the Lord's, and the fullness thereof; the world, and they that dwell therein* (Psalm 24:1).

Paul was an experienced seaman, having had many journeys by treacherous waters. In fact, he was a man acquainted with perilous situations.

As a young man, he had actively persecuted members of an up and coming sect who claimed that Jesus Christ was their Messiah. He witnessed and even cheered onward the stoning of Stephen, the first person in the New Testament to give his life for the cause of Christ.

> *And Saul was [not only] consenting to [Stephen's] death [he was pleased and entirely approving]. On that day a great and severe persecution broke out against the church which was in Jerusalem; and they were all scattered throughout the regions of Judea and Samaria, except the apostles (special messengers)* (Acts 8:1 AMP).

Paul, then known as Saul, was violent in his persecution of Christians, both men and women.

> *But Saul shamefully treated and laid waste the church continuously [with cruelty and violence]; and entering house after house, he dragged out men and women and committed them to prison* (Acts 8:3 AMP).

He was full of murderous threats against Christians.

> *Meanwhile Saul, still drawing his breath hard from threatening and murderous desire against the disciples of the Lord, went to the high priest* (Acts 9:1 AMP).

After his miraculous conversion, the Jews plotted to assassinate Paul because of his conversion to Christ.

He Was Stoned, Left For Dead

But some Jews arrived there from Antioch and Iconium; and having persuaded the people and won them over, they stoned Paul and [afterward] dragged him out of the town, thinking that he was dead (Acts 14:19 AMP).

Once, he escaped over a wall in a basket. He was arrested, brought before King Agrippa, escaped riots at Ephesus, endured false brethren, suffered shipwrecks, endured hunger and thirst, and had a resume of suffering as an apostle of the Lord. This man was accustomed to storms, hardships, difficulties, adversities, and suffering. He was extremely familiar with the Mediterranean, having logged more than 3,500 miles by sea.

However, as a prisoner on board this particular sailing vessel in Acts 27, all hope was gone. There was no way, naturally speaking, for Paul or any of those on board to make it out of this killer hurricane alive. This one was called "Euroclydon" (see Acts 27:140). This was the storm that every sailor feared and dreaded. It would be destructive. This was the absolute end.

There Was No Hope

Have you already been through so much, only to realize that you are back in the rigors of battle again? Have you had one date with disaster after another and now here comes the *"real battle"* after the battle? Many things can try to take you out.

- Divorce
- Bankruptcy
- The loss of a child
- The loss of a job
- The loss of your spouse
- Terminal illness
- A dreaded diagnosis
- Rejection
- Betrayal
- Sabotage
- Legal battles
- A prison sentence
- The loss of a relationship
- Emotional stress
- Trouble in your home

These are the kinds of things that drive us to our knees. That is the best place to be!

Now the God of hope fill you with all joy and peace in believing, that ye may abound in hope, through the power of the Holy Ghost (Romans 15:13).

Remind all of your troubles that God is the God of all hope. And remind yourself that His hope abides.

Paul Had No Direction During Disaster

And when neither sun nor stars in many days appeared, and no small tempest lay on us, all hope that we should be saved was then taken away (Acts 27:20).

Remember: To a sailor, the sun and the stars were the compass points, the tools of navigation. For Paul and all on board, there was no sense of direction once the sun and stars were hidden.

I know that you need an awareness of direction in your life, even in the middle of the storms of life. Even here, God has still promised to lead us. Your storm never stops the general direction of the move of God. You might not have specific details, but that doesn't mean that you have to lie down and die. You can still move toward your victory, your wholeness, your destiny, His plan, His purposes. You do not have to stagnate, even in the middle of the most ferocious trials of life.

Walking through one tragedy after another, I felt as if the magnetic pole of my earth shifted, and I could not tell up from down, east from west. I was directionless.

"Lord, this is killing me. I can't sense Your direction at all," I poured out my heart.

That is when I heard Him say, "If you don't know where I'm leading, go by My leaning." I heard Him speak to my heart, "Do you know the things I already like?"

"Yes, Lord, of course, I do. Your Word tells me about You," I instinctively replied.

"Then start doing the things you already know that I like," He gently stated. My direction began to change when I started leaning. Lean your heart in the direction of God's heart.

Abraham went out. He did not have the details. He just began to lean. He knew where he couldn't stay. Some of you cannot stay in a place that is continually bringing you down, taking the life of God out of you and robbing you of your destiny in the Lord. You have to leave that environment—even if you don't have it all together. You do not have to wait until you get it all together for God to move for you.

The good Samaritan (see Luke 10) poured in the oil and wine right there on the Jericho road, and then he put the wounded man on his own beast. He did not wait until things got better. He did something right then and there. Lean in the direction that you already know God leans toward.

The woman with the issue of blood (see Mark 5) went toward Jesus. She didn't have specific leadings. She had just heard of Him and went in His direction.

God's promise to guide you has not been voided by your trials:

By Your words I can see where I'm going; they throw a beam of light on my dark path. I've committed myself and I'll never turn back from living by Your righteous order. Everything's falling apart on me, GOD; put me together again with Your Word (Psalm 119:105-107 MSG).

Your darkest days can still produce something for Him. After my husband went home to be with the Lord, I told the Lord, "Lord, if You are through, I am through." I did not know how I could go on from that point.

He simply said, "I'm not through." I began to take baby steps in the dark. You can't go fast when your life is like this, but I can promise you one thing—*it is not your time to die!*

When in the storm, return to prayer. Paul began to "incubate" hope through prayer. A Bible student of mine, who happened to be a scientist, heard me say that "prayer is the incubator of hope." Being in the lab most of the day, she immediately had a visual of what this meant. To her, it meant rapid, exponential growth, as she had seen cells multiply quickly in the incubators in the laboratory.

An *incubator* is a chamber "used to provide controlled environmental conditions…for…cultivation."[1] Paul went to this incubator called prayer, and God brought hope into a hopeless circumstance. Not only for Paul, but for every prisoner and crew member on board.

But after long abstinence Paul stood forth in the midst of them, and said, Sirs, ye should have hearkened unto me, and not have loosed from Crete, and to have gained this harm and loss. And now I exhort you to be of good cheer: for there shall be no loss of any man's life among you, but of the ship. For there stood by me this night the angel of God, whose I am, and whom I serve, saying, Fear not, Paul; thou must be brought before Caesar: and, lo, God hath given thee all them that sail with thee. Wherefore, sirs, be of good cheer: for I believe God, that it shall be even as it was told me (Acts 27:21-25).

Paul knew that the anchor of his soul was a far greater anchor than the one on the ship. Hope is the soul's anchor in the most turbulent storms of life.

> *[Now] we have this [hope] as a sure and steadfast anchor of the soul [it cannot slip and it cannot break down under whoever steps out upon it—a hope] that reaches farther and enters into [the very certainty of the Presence] within the veil...* (Hebrews 6:19 AMP).

You might be in such a storm that all hope is gone and your compass is spinning. Your days might be spent shrouded in pain. Let me encourage you: there is restoration for you. He is such a grace-filled, mercy-filled, hope-filled God!

> *Is there no balm in Gilead? Is there no physician there? Why then is not the health of the daughter of my people restored? [Because Zion no longer enjoyed the presence of the Great Physician!]* (Jeremiah 8:22 AMP)

Jesus is our Healer; He is the balm for our troubled lives. He is our Great Physician. He can heal your broken heart and life. He is the One who will walk through the rubble with you. He is the Restorer of broken-down lives. Jesus is still our hope.

> *Paul, an apostle of Jesus Christ by the commandment of God our Saviour, and Lord Jesus Christ, which is our hope...* (1 Timothy 1:1).

Not only did Paul make it through alive, but everyone on board was spared, even when the crewmates wanted to kill all the prisoners. The Word of the Lord was fulfilled in detail.

Last night God's angel stood at my side, an angel of this God I serve, saying to me, "Don't give up, Paul. You're going to stand before Caesar yet—and everyone sailing with you is also going to make it." So, dear friends, take heart. I believe God will do exactly what He told me. But we're going to shipwreck on some island or other (Acts 27:23-26 MSG).

God's Word Never Fails

Then Paul ministered on the island of Malta in the very spot where the storm had so mercilessly spit them out. In fact, this place that could have been their death became their place of provision. The islanders loaded them down with goods! A strong center of Christianity was established on the island as a result of the storm. Your storm can work for your good and for God's glory.

And it came to pass, that the father of Publius lay sick of a fever and of a bloody flux: to whom Paul entered in, and prayed, and laid his hands on him, and healed him. So when this was done, others also, which had diseases in the island, came, and were healed: who also honoured us with many honours; and when we departed, they laded us with such things as were necessary (Acts 28:8-10).

Whatever it is you are facing, let me encourage you that God knows the end from the beginning. There is a plan that God is working, even when we do not see Him at work. He is recalibrating us.

If people, places, and things are shifting from your life, God still knows the way that you are taking. He is about to give you an unrelenting sense of His destiny for your life!

But he knoweth the way that I take: when he hath tried me, I shall come forth as gold (Job 23:10).

Who are kept by the power of God through faith unto salvation ready to be revealed in the last time. Wherein ye greatly rejoice, though now for a season, if need be, ye are in heaviness through manifold temptations: that the trial of your faith, being much more precious than of gold that perisheth, though it be tried with fire, might be found unto praise and honour and glory at the appearing of Jesus Christ... (1 Peter 1:5-7).

Shattered Dreams? God's Still There

Joseph, the favorite son of Jacob, was a dreamer. His dreams came from God. His dreams also got him into trouble with his brothers, who dumped him into a pit, sold him into slavery, and led their heartbroken father to believe that Joseph had been killed by a wild animal (see Gen. 37).

Joseph's story is one of extreme emotion and suspense, heartache and restoration. Joseph was rejected, betrayed, and alone—separated from his family, and especially his beloved father, for many years.

What do you do when you lose your own loved ones to betrayal? What do you do when a pit has been dug and you are in it? What do you do when your dreams have been mocked by the very people who should believe in you and cheer you on? What do you do when you have been forgotten and forsaken by people who should love you to the end? What do you do when even God seems to have left you to die in your misery?

You must be honest with your pain if you are going to be honest with your recovery. If you are not honest with the pain, you will not be honest with the recovery. If you mask the pain, you will mask the recovery.

God wants you totally whole; there is no need to put a bandage on a cancer. God knows the difference. Your wholeness is vital to your effectiveness and enjoyment of life. No situation has the power to destroy you. This message is for you right now.

After Bill's death, as I would drive down the highway day after day with hot tears streaming onto my clothes, I would question God about my own painful situations. "Why?" That is all I wanted to know. "God, can You please help me to understand Your ways in all of this?"

All I could faintly hear Him say was, "I've got the big picture."

God calls on us to trust Him. This is what I call faith's graduation. There was a day in my life when my faith graduated to trust.

This is what happened in the story of Joseph. All of his intentions of being a dream-builder were going to have to fall on the One who gave the dreams in the first place. He would be in situation after situation that required trust in God, even when he couldn't trace Him. We learn to trust God in the hardest of times.

We trust that God knows what is best and that whatever it takes for Him to work that out, He will do it.

Young Joseph went through setup after setup that put him in positions where he had to depend on God. God was teaching him that his total reliance was to be solely upon the Lord. Time after time, Joseph was put into circumstances where there was no way to win. God was getting him ready to rise to power. But he would have to walk through unbearable process after process before it was all over.

One of the primary lessons that we learn from the life of Joseph is that, when our dreams are all shattered, God has not left us, and He is providentially working on our behalf, even when we are not aware of it.

God has not abandoned us. People might have walked out, but that is when God specializes in walking in. The baker and the butler forgot about Joseph. When others walk out, God walks in. God is always mindful of our struggles, always alert to our heart's cry.

Jacob, Joseph's father, had a life filled with trickery, deceit, and jealousy. He also headed a home that was rife with an atmosphere of relational competition. Out of that mess, somehow a pure diamond in the rough, Joseph, emerged. Innocently, Joseph became the favored son among his 11 brothers. It wasn't his fault that his aging father doted on him each and every day. This fondness would cost Joseph. His favored position might even have led Joseph to tell his brothers of the dream he had. What was the dream?

> *And Joseph dreamed a dream, and he told it his brethren: and they hated him yet the more. And he said unto them, Hear, I pray you, this dream which I have dreamed: for, behold, we were binding sheaves in the field, and, lo, my sheaf arose, and also stood upright; and, behold, your sheaves stood round about, and made obeisance to my sheaf. And his brethren said to him, Shalt thou indeed reign over us? or shalt thou indeed have dominion over us? And they hated him yet the more for his dreams, and for his words. And he dreamed yet another dream, and told it his brethren, and*

said, Behold, I have dreamed a dream more; and, behold, the sun and the moon and the eleven stars made obeisance to me (Genesis 37:5-9).

The only thing Joseph really left out was the simple phrase, "And, oh yes, by the way, you guys will bow down to me one day." But that is exactly what he meant.

This brazen display of the dream was more than the already-hot-with-jealousy brothers could stand. They plotted against him when they saw him coming to them in the field.

And they said one to another, Behold, this dreamer cometh. Come now therefore, and let us slay him, and cast him into some pit, and we will say, Some evil beast hath devoured him: and we shall see what will become of his dreams. And Reuben heard it, and he delivered him out of their hands; and said, Let us not kill him. And Reuben said unto them, Shed no blood, but cast him into this pit that is in the wilderness, and lay no hand upon him; that he might rid him out of their hands, to deliver him to his father again. And it came to pass, when Joseph was come unto his brethren, that they stript Joseph out of his coat, his coat of many colours that was on him; and they took him, and cast him into a pit: and the pit was empty, there was no water in it (Genesis 37:19-24).

From this place of emptiness, betrayal, love lost, dreams shattered, hope would seem to be millions of miles away for Joseph.

Isolation can be a call to prayer. I have no doubt that from this lonely, secluded, out-of-the-way, isolated pit, Joseph began to pray.

Joseph was heartlessly sold into an Ishmaelite caravan and went on to become the property of Potiphar, a high-ranking official in Pharaoh's army.

What a system shock to be forced to start a new life. Joseph came from a home where his father treated him with specialties every day. Now, he had to learn a new way to live.

My son and I experienced this when my husband died. We didn't know what to expect of our life without "Dad." When your spouse dies, the life that you knew dies as well. You have to start a new life; you have to learn your new life and where and how you now fit in.

Joseph's emotional state of being can only be vaguely imagined. Some of you have had your highest and best dreams shattered and you have had to bravely start new lives. Courage had to be summoned in order to carry on with this thing that we call *life*.

Robert Frost said, "I can sum up everything I've ever learned about life in three words...it goes on."[2] And so life does. We must trust that our times of trials will only make us more like Him and better servants to others. We must forge forward through every circumstance of life. We must trust again. We must hope again. Life goes on.

In the house of Potiphar, Joseph would quickly advance because of his heart of integrity and his excellent servanthood. He had no way of knowing that he was in for another sabotage of his dream that would put him in a different kind of pit, one called *prison*.

*And it came to pass from the time that he had made him overseer
in his house, and over all that he had, that the Lord blessed the*

Egyptian's house for Joseph's sake; and the blessing of the Lord was upon all that he had in the house, and in the field. And he left all that he had in Joseph's hand; and he knew not ought he had, save the bread which he did eat. And Joseph was a goodly person, and well favoured. And it came to pass after these things, that his master's wife cast her eyes upon Joseph; and she said, Lie with me. But he refused, and said unto his master's wife, Behold, my master wotteth not what is with me in the house, and he hath committed all that he hath to my hand; there is none greater in this house than I; neither hath he kept back any thing from me but thee, because thou art his wife: how then can I do this great wickedness, and sin against God? And it came to pass, as she spake to Joseph day by day, that he hearkened not unto her, to lie by her, or to be with her. And it came to pass about this time, that Joseph went into the house to do his business; and there was none of the men of the house there within. And she caught him by his garment, saying, Lie with me: and he left his garment in her hand, and fled, and got him out. And it came to pass, when she saw that he had left his garment in her hand, and was fled forth, that she called unto the men of her house, and spake unto them, saying, See, he hath brought in an Hebrew unto us to mock us; he came in unto me to lie with me, and I cried with a loud voice: and it came to pass, when he heard that I lifted up my voice and cried, that he left his garment with me, and fled, and got him out. And she laid up his garment by her, until his lord came home. And she spake unto him according to these words, saying, The Hebrew servant, which thou hast brought unto us, came in unto me to mock me: and it came to pass, as I lifted up my voice and cried, that he left his garment with me, and fled out. And it came to pass, when his master heard the words of his wife, which she spake unto him, saying, After this manner did thy servant to me; that his wrath was kindled. And Joseph's master took him, and put him into the prison, a place where the king's prisoners were bound: and he was there in the prison (Genesis 39:5-20).

After Potiphar's wife unjustly accused Joseph, he was allowed to live, but only in a prison. From this depressing place, Joseph would, once again, be sorely tested. Sleeping for many years, on a mat more than likely stained with blood, urine, feces, and vomit, Joseph would once again find favor. Little did he know that he was about to get off of life's floor permanently.

Joseph was imprisoned for a crime he did not commit, but God had not forgotten Joseph. In fact, Joseph was unknowingly being put into position so that every single dream God had ever given him would come to pass. I know you feel like quitting, but it's too soon for you to quit now! For all you know, the very thing you thought would kill you, might actually position you for greater effectiveness. Sometimes, a closed door is the best thing in the world for us.

After almost 13 years, God was about to move on Joseph's behalf—*big time!* All of the adversities of life had served to position him for the fulfillment of the dreams God had given him.

You might have felt "stuck." Even now, you might feel that what life has promised has failed miserably. Let Joseph's story give you hope. You do not have to live an imitation life; you can live the abundant life Christ has already provided. This is your hour to arise! You have been processed.

You have paid a high, high price to be in this place of release. Just as Joseph was released from prison after an "overnight" stay of 13 years, in one day, your life can be changed from hopelessness to ever-increasing joy.

Joseph was favored, even when he didn't know it. He was favored even when every situation of his life challenged God's manifested favor. You are favored even when you don't feel like it. You are favored when others say you are not. No one can decide the ultimate will of God for your life. You can choose your attitude in this trial. God's grace abounds where sins, shortcomings, mishaps, and confusion abound. God's grace abounds where need of any kind exists.

> *Let us then fearlessly and confidently and boldly draw near to the throne of grace (the throne of God's unmerited favor to us sinners), that we may receive mercy [for our failures] and find grace to help in good time for every need [appropriate help and well-timed help, coming just when we need it]* (Hebrews 4:16 AMP).

As God continued to give Joseph favor, he was put in charge of other prisoners. Included among them were a baker and a butler. On the same night, these two men had dreams (see Gen. 40). Joseph offered to help them; he told them that God was the interpreter of dreams.

Joseph gave them the meanings of their dreams with perfect accuracy. The butler would be released from prison in three days and be restored to his job in Pharaoh's house. Joseph also asked this butler if he would explain his plight of false accusation and false imprisonment to Pharaoh. Perhaps, Joseph believed that he, too, would soon be getting out of prison.

Joseph went on to tell the chief baker that in three days, he would be hanged. Just as Joseph interpreted, the butler was released back into commission in Pharaoh's courts, and the chief baker was executed. All of this occurred within the three-day time period.

God had his hand on Joseph. He was able to help others with their dreams. He waited patiently for the prison doors to swing open for him, because the butler had promised to help him. Regrettably, sometimes, the very ones we help to achieve their dreams later refuse to help us with ours.

Two long, hard years went by. Joseph was, no doubt, heartsick. Hope had once again been delayed.

Unrelenting disappointment leaves you heartsick... (Proverbs 13:12 MSG).

He had faced overwhelming disappointment after disappointment.

Let me encourage you that disappointments cannot destroy you. They will strengthen, intensify, and temper you, but they cannot destroy you.

The measure of your success in life is related directly to your ability to handle disappointment.

The Rev. Martin Luther King, Jr., the great civil-rights advocate, said, "We must accept infinite disappointment, but never lose infinite hope."[3]

Disappointment is defined as "the act or an instance of disappointing: the state or emotion of being disappointed."[4] It is "the act of disappointing, or the state of being disappointed; defeat or failure of expectation or hope; miscarriage of design or plan; frustration."[5]

Joseph's dreams had been miscarried over and over again. But even though the butler had forgotten Joseph, God knew exactly where he was and what was going to happen next. It was all a setup.

Two years later, Pharaoh dreamed two different dreams. The chief butler all of a sudden remembered that, while he was in prison, a young man named Joseph accurately interpreted dreams.

Pharaoh called for Joseph. Joseph approached Pharaoh clean-shaven and in appropriate attire. Joseph explained that Pharaoh's dreams foretold a famine that would be preceded by seven years of plenty. Joseph told Pharaoh that, during the years of plenty, preparation would have to be made for the lean years. Joseph also took the liberty to wisely suggest that a man of wisdom be appointed to oversee the entire operation of food conservation and distribution.

> So now let Pharaoh seek out and provide a man discreet, understanding, proficient, and wise and set him over the land of Egypt [as governor] (Genesis 41:33 AMP).

Positioned for Change

I like to think that Joseph was actually suggesting himself for the overseer's position. After all, who was better trained to endure all kinds of pressure, time restrictions, people's expectations, etc.? Who had been better prepared to face demands and anxieties?

God had prepared Joseph in the most complex of environments. He had thoroughly sent His chosen servant through the rigors of mental toughness and skill to survive the hardest of times. Joseph was ready for such an assignment.

Pharaoh saw that Joseph was full of the Spirit of God and, in that moment, elevated Joseph, a common prisoner, to the position of governor of all the land. Instantly, Joseph had become second-in-command to Pharaoh himself!

Finally, Joseph was about to walk into his dream. All of life's disappointments, all of the heartache and betrayal, all of the loneliness and misunderstandings, were about to be recompensed. Even the loss of his family, the cruelty of his brothers, and the heartbreak of his aging father were about to be dealt with.

Joseph's brothers, who had meant it all for evil, were afraid of Joseph when they discovered who he had become. But Joseph understood that God had meant all the hardship for good. He reassured his brothers that he would not retaliate for their betrayal of him.

> *Joseph replied, "Don't be afraid. Do I act for God? Don't you see, you planned evil against me but God used those same plans for my good, as you see all around you right now—life for many people. Easy now, you have nothing to fear; I'll take care of you and your children." He reassured them, speaking with them heart-to-heart* (Genesis 50:19-21 MSG).

God will far surpass all of your expectations if you will only let Him do it His way. God has a plan for your life that will go beyond anything that you can ever dream or imagine. Quitting is not your destiny. In fact, you have just been positioned to hope again.

Now to Him Who, by (in consequence of) the [action of His] power that is at work within us, is able to [carry out His purpose and] do superabundantly, far over and above all that we [dare] ask or think [infinitely beyond our highest prayers, desires, thoughts, hopes, or dreams] (Ephesians 3:20 AMP).

Restored Hope Renews Purpose

From this moment, you can live a life motivated by purpose. Let me give you five hope statements relating to your purpose:

- ❧ God assigned you a specific purpose even before you were born.
- ❧ All the people, places, things, and ideas you need for His purposes are coming into your life.
- ❧ You have the personal privilege and responsibility of discovering your unique purpose.
- ❧ Sharing your purpose with others creates intensity.
- ❧ You are designed to live by vision.

God has a plan for your life, and the Holy Spirit will not rest until it is fulfilled. The Holy Spirit is aggressive, passionate, and relentless when it comes to your purpose in life.

For everything there is a season… (Ecclesiastes 3:1).

Abraham Lincoln said, "You can have anything you want—if you want it badly enough. You can be anything you want to be, do anything you set out to accomplish if you hold to that desire with singleness of purpose."[6]

The great motivator Anthony Robbins said:

Goals are a means to an end, not the ultimate purpose of our lives. They are simply a tool to concentrate our focus and move us in a direction. The only reason we really pursue goals is to cause ourselves to expand and grow. Achieving goals by themselves will never make us happy in the long term; it's who you become, as you overcome the obstacles necessary to achieve your goals, that can give you the deepest and most long-lasting sense of fulfillment.[7]

Your whole journey has been an education in who God really meant for you to be. It is not just about the destination, but about what happens inside of us along the way.

You see, we all came into this world with nothing, and the purpose of life is to make something out of nothing. Purpose is intrinsically linked to fulfillment. For the Christian to be fulfilled and not stagnant, purpose must continually be turned upward and outward. The Holy Spirit turns victims into victors. We receive His healing for our broken, wounded places and then we go on to fulfill God's purpose and destiny for our lives.

A strong life is not just wishes and intentions, but purpose and hope coupled with positive performance. Many people spend their days settling for a lifetime in the rocking chair of mediocrity when it is so much better to go after your passion with gusto.

What is your passion? What does your heart lean toward? Sometimes, we just have to slow down, get all of the extra static out of our lives, and listen to our hearts.

It has been said that God gives every bird a worm, but He does not throw it in the nest. You have to go for your purpose in life. People who have been thrown into hopeless situations and have come out, not just surviving, but thriving, can be the very best at life's purpose. It is people like you and me who have the greatest appreciation for life and for an opportunity to fulfill our lives with God's purpose in mind.

Have you ever noticed that people who have been given second chances at life seem to embrace life with every ounce of their strength and relish each day as a gift from the Lord? Life *is* such a precious gift.

Now that we have survived and now that we have come through the worst storms of our lives, we are now ready to pour sacrificially and generously into God's Kingdom purpose for our lives. Deep down in your heart and soul, you are now ready to tap into God's magnanimous reservoirs of hope and dispense it unreservedly to others. Is there a need to hesitate when you have been given the gift of hope to give without restraint?

What's wrong with hoping again? What's wrong with believing again? What's wrong with trusting again? Get your eyes out of the rear view mirror and start looking out of the windshield. You have had so many opportunities to quit, throw in the towel, give up, and fall back. You have already overcome challenges that would take most people out of life's game—but you are still in. There is a purpose to all of this!

God has called you to your *now* and to your future. You have been placed on this earth by your Creator who has nothing but the best in

His heart for you. Each day holds new opportunities to explore God's purpose without limits.

Lance Armstrong, a cancer survivor, said, "I take nothing for granted. I now have only good days, or great days."[7]

The rest of your life is the best of your life! Act as though it were impossible to fail. God knows how to take every ruined and wasted dream and compensate for all of your losses.

…Weeping may endure for a night, but joy cometh in the morning (Psalm 30:5).

Because of your newly grounded hope, you never have to face devastation again—even though you will face disappointments! Your hope is anchored. And what makes it so immovable as an anchor? Because of what holds the anchor! We are attached to Christ Jesus, our Rock! Our Hope is in Christ, and our Hope is Christ! Hope thrives in the God Zone!

Which hope we have as an anchor of the soul, both sure and stedfast (Hebrews 6:19).

Expectancy is here.

Return to your fortress, O prisoners of hope; even now I announce that I will restore twice as much to you (Zechariah 9:12 NIV).

It's time to step into the *now* phase of your life. Your future is waiting.

Endnotes

1. Merriam-Webster Online Dictionary. 2009, s.v. "incubator," http://www.merriam-webster.com/dictionary/incubator (accessed December 21, 2009).

2. http://quotationsbook.com/quote/19455/.

3. Merriam-Webster Online Dictionary. 2009, s.v. "disappointment," http://www.merriam-webster.com/dictionary/disappointment (accessed December 21, 2009).

4. http://onlinedictionary.datasegment.com/word/disappointment.

5. http://thinkexist.com/quotes/abraham_lincoln/4.html.

6. http://www.famous-quotes.com/author.php?aid=6162.

7. http://quotations.about.com/cs/inspirationquotes/a/Attitude21.htm

Hope
Journal

Hope Journal

Hope
Journal

Finding the GOD ZONE

Study Guide

JANA ALCORN

Table of Contents

Introduction

"Hope deferred makes the heart sick, but when the desire comes, it is a tree of life" (Proverbs 13:12 NKJV).

This study guide was written so that you might gain a deeper understanding of the principles of hope and activate them in your daily life.

To effectively use this Study Guide, read the corresponding chapter in *Finding the God Zone*. Then complete a thorough reading of the Scriptures designated and answer the Study Guide questions by referring back to the chapter. Afterward, you can check your answers using the Answer Guide in the back of the book.

You will see that a quote from each chapter is included at the beginning of each lesson. I encourage you to use these Hope Quotes as discussion starters when you are in group studies. In addition, I have included more than 100 empowering Scripture verses at the conclusion to further engage your journey to accelerated hope in Christ Jesus. Repeat them aloud several times each day. Meditate upon them and take action. In addition, you might also want to journal your thoughts and inspirations as you progress in His hopes for your life.

If you will patiently, persistently, and meditatively work through this book, you will discover the transforming power of renewed expectations. Anticipation is about to abound in your life!

Millions of people suffer daily from hopelessness, broken dreams, unfulfilled expectations, and abandonment of purpose. I have great news from the Word of God and from the Holy Spirit. You don't have to live a life of regrets, reserve, and retreat!

I pray that as you work through the Study Guide and book chapters, you will once again understand God's immeasurable love and hope for your life.

Let Your mercy and loving-kindness, O Lord, be upon us, in pro-portion to our waiting and hoping for You (Psalm 33:22 AMP).

CHAPTER ONE

There Really Is a God Zone!

"Yes, God does exist. Yes, He is real, and yes, He does love me."

1. The God Zone will establish three things:
   a) God does _____.
   b) God is _____.
   c) He _____ me.

2. Read Job 19:14-25.

   _____ was a man whose trials made him a legend.

3. Job knew there was a _____ _____ even though Job felt himself devoid of God's _____ _____ many days.

4. Because Job had a core belief in the God Zone, he was able to _____, in spite of feelings of depression, loneliness, betrayal, rejection, etc....

"I _____ that my Redeemer _____"! (Job 19:25)

5. This core belief in the God Zone will be your first breeding ground for _____.

6. Hope is always nurtured by _____.

7. _____ is the breeding ground for hope.

8. Prayer is the _____ place for hope and hope is the _____ of _____.

9. Write out Romans 15:13 in your favorite translation.

    _____

    _____

    _____

    _____

Within each of us lies the desire to connect with our Creator in a very personal way.

10. Read Esther Chapter 4.

    When Esther faced the annihilation of her people and there seemed to be _____ hope, she ran to the place of _____.

11. Prayer is the _____ _____ of hope.

12. Prayer is _____ to _____ as you would talk to your best friend.

13. Prayer is "the _____ of the _____ toward God."

14. Read Hebrews 7:25 in the Amplified Bible. According to this verse, _____ is always _____ and intervening on our behalf.

15. God knows your place of _____.

16. Read Romans 8:24-28.
    The Holy Spirit is well able to take our cries before the throne of God's _____.

17. One of the meanings of intercession is "to _____ _____."

18. Intercession means:
    a) _____ _____ _____
    b) _____ _____ _____ _____ _____
    c) _____ _____ _____
    d) _____ _____

19. _____ is one of the highest forms of prayer.

20. Intercession allows you to:
    a) _____ _____
    b) _____ _____ _____ _____
    c) _____ _____ _____ _____ _____

    _____ _____.

21. Exodus 2:23 describes the _____ cry of the Israelites to God.

This level of crying is usually born out of life's most

_____ _____.

22. God does not forget our _____ and there is a _____ that God _____ refuse.

23. Birth pangs always come _____ birth.

24. Read Job 13:15.

God wants to graduate your _____ to _____.

*P*rayer *is the conception chamber of hope*
for your tomorrows, and it will breed faith for
your todays.

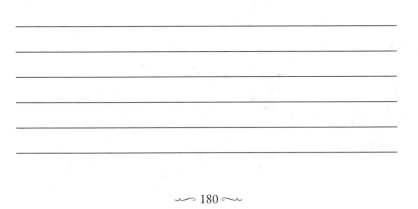

Digging Deeper Into Hope—

Read and discuss the Hope Quote at the beginning of this chapter of the Study Guide. Has there ever been a time that you doubted the existence of God? Have you ever wavered in the fact of His unconditional love for you? What can you do to strengthen your basic foundation in Christ?

_____

_____

_____

_____

_____

_____

Hope in Action—

Write down three things that you will do today to increase your hope in Him!

_____

_____

_____

_____

_____

_____

_____

_____

_____

_____

_____

_____

Chapter Two

This Is Working for You

"Whatever your design, God has made you for your assignment."

1. Write out Second Corinthians 4:17.

    _____

    _____

    _____

    _____

2. In the midst of what you think is the end, you will find what is really

    the _____.

3. Your _____ is a _____.

4. Read First Corinthians 15:14.

    The _____ looked so opposed to God's intentions for after
    the resurrection.

5. Do not insult the _____ of God by judging yourself on the basis of where you are now.

6. If you have been through a "crucifixion experience," don't _____ now!

7. Read Ephesians 6:12.
   You must learn to deal with high-level _____ forces that come against your _____ in order to achieve God's destiny for your life.

God's divine intention for you is so great!

8. Prepare for what _____ has in mind, not what you have in mind.

9. You need to _____: God has written my name on _____ _____, signed it in the _____ of Jesus, and _____ weapon formed can ever possibly prosper.

10. God has made you for your _____.

11. Start asking yourself the right questions:
    a) Am I here because of _____ and _____?
    b) Am I here because of a _____ of _____?
    c) Am I here because God alone knows, that _____ _____ _____, I can get to where _____ _____ to take me for His glory?

12. You might have a great _____, but God wants to make you a great _____.

13. Your _____ reveals you.

14. Read Romans 4:17-21.
God had _____ and _____ for Abraham to father a son.

15. Abraham's hope had been _____ because the promise seemed to be _____.

16. Yet, Abraham believed God and believed in _____ against _____.

17. When God makes a promise to our lives, it is _____ up to us to fulfill it.

18. Beelzebub translated in the Greek, means "lord of the _____."

19. This name gives us insight into the _____ of satan and his demons.

20. As is the case with flies:
a) They are _____ of disease.
b) They _____ quickly, given the right environ-ment.
c) They _____ all territories.
d) They are _____ to junk, garbage, and trash.

21. If we have _____ _____ that have pro-duced bitterness, resentment, revenge, jealousies, etc., we become breeding grounds of demonic activity.

22. If we have "_____" in our lives—the _____ that we hold onto, the _____ of which the Holy Spirit convicts us of—we become places of demonic interest.

23. Read Romans 12:11 (AMP).
    God's Word tells us to be burning, _____ _____, ablaze with the Holy Spirit's power in our lives.

24. Demonic spirits live in a realm of _____ and _____.

25. _____ is the emotion of hell.

26. A person cannot live without _____.

27. You have a _____ in life; you have a divine _____!

28. Write out Romans 8:37.

    _____

    _____

    _____

    _____

    _____

    _____

*W*hat God wants is our openness and
submissiveness to His divine possibilities. Will
you trust Him?

C–

Digging Deeper Into Hope—

Read and discuss the Hope Quote at the beginning of this chapter of the Study Guide. What are some of the clear assignments that God has given you? Recall how God used imperfect people to achieve remarkable things. What are ways to build your confidence in God?

_____

_____

_____

_____

_____

_____

Hope in Action—

Do one thing today that will build confidence in your willingness to be used by God.

_____

_____

_____

CHAPTER THREE

This Is Bigger Than You

"When we are born again, we start a new life, a life that connects to a higher cause and purpose."

1. Now that we are born again, we now connect to the _____ of _____ and to all the _____ of the _____ of God in our lives, even when we do not know or understand what that might be or what it might mean.

2. We all have an _____.

3. It is like the Greek athletes who were each given a _____ to run in.

4. If you don't _____, you will make it through this season of your life.

5. Refuse to be _____. Stay in your _____.

6. Read Exodus 30:22-32.
   In the Old Testament, those things that were going to be used in the service of the sanctuary had to be anointed with _____.

7. The ingredients had to be _____ and carefully measured.

8. Interestingly, one of the five ingredients was _____.

9. Myrrh is very _____.

10. There could be no _____ _____ without myrrh.

11. The very thing that the enemy thought would take you out, is the thing that is _____ the oil of God's anointing into and through your life!

12. This anointing process is going to be the catalyst that will _____ your purpose.

13. You have been _____ and _____ by the Master.

14. You will carry out your assignment because of the _____ in and upon your life.

15. The storms of our lives are _____.

16. We cannot choose our _____, but we can choose our _____ _____.

17. God will use events of our lives to _____ _____ in us so that we can have _____.

Most often, it is the pressures and the struggles of life that do more to strengthen us....

18. God forges His chosen vessels in the place of _____ _____.

19. Read First Corinthians 3:10-11.

    The difference in your life will be the _____ that you have laid.

20. Any house that is built upon _____ will withstand storms.

21. You will also stand firmly during this time of trial if your feet are planted firmly upon the Rock, _____ _____.

22. Name the six main ways in which you will face trying storms:

    a) _____

    b) _____

    c) _____

    d) _____

    e) _____

    f) _____

23. Read Acts 27:9-41.

    To a sailor, if you have no sun or stars, you have no _____ or bearings because you have no compass points from which to navigate.

24. In the storm, Paul went to _____.

25. _____is the environment in which hope can grow.

26. If you are walking through the ferocious storms of life, it is time to
_____.

27. Prayer changes your _____ about your trial.

28. God can handle your _____.

29. Prayer _____ _____ _____ away from the natural circumstances and onto the promises of God's Word.

30. Write out John 16:33.

_____

_____

_____

_____

_____

*Everyone who hears these words of Mine and
acts on them, may be compared to a wise man
who built his house on the rock*
(Matthew 7:24 NASB).

Digging Deeper Into Hope—

Read and discuss the Hope Quote at the beginning of this chapter of the Study Guide. Have you ever thought there was a specific purpose to your life? Does God have a plan for every single person?

_____

_____

_____

_____

_____

_____

_____

_____

_____

Hope in Action—

Talk to someone today about God's purposes and plans for your life.

_____

_____

_____

_____

CHAPTER FOUR

Expectation Is a Law

"The strength of my position is always in Christ."

1. Your _____ can live again.

2. Your _____ can soar again.

3. You can _____ again!

4. The acronym H.O.P.E. stands for:

   H _____

   O _____

   P _____

   E _____

5. Now is the time to _____ and _____.

6. Even if you have lost _____, they have not been lost to God.

7. God is in the _____ business.

8. From the list of "in Christ" Scripture, select two that best state what Christ means to you:

    a) _____

    b) _____

9. Jesus did not come to _____ _____ up.

10. He came to make you _____.

11. Just as there has been _____, _____ now begins.

12. Write out Luke 4:18 from the Amplified Bible.

    _____

    _____

    _____

    _____

13. If you have been _____ _____ through calamities, your situation is perfect for God.

14. Read Isaiah 61:3.

    He really will give you _____ for _____ from a burned-out life.

15. In the Bible, the Holy Spirit and the Word of God are very sensitive and tender to _____ people.

16. Our _____ wounds and bruises are just as real as the physical ones, but the hurt they cause us is far greater.

*For we do not have a High Priest Who is unable
to understand and sympathize and have a shared
feeling with our weaknesses and infirmities...*
(Hebrews 4:15 AMP).

17. Jesus understands your struggles and is always moved with

    _____.

18. Read Ephesians 1:3-6.

    You will never shock God by the "_____" of your life....
    He *chose* you _____ you walked in any decision-making
    ability for your life.

19. Let Him speak to the _____ place.

20. Let Him come in to the place that you have _____.

21. God's first _____ about you is His final _____!

22. Read Mark 5:35-42.

    In the Gospels there is a story of a little girl who tragically

    _____.

23. But do you know what Jesus did? Jesus _____ anyway.

24. Her story was _____ _____.

25. Jesus comes to your _____ even when they are already

    _____.

26. Your situation is _____ for Him.

27. You are free to move into a life of clear, positive _____ rather than negative ones blurred by misplaced _____ or unmet expectations.

28. _____ or _____ expectations can lead our lives in the wrong direction.

29. When expectations are not met, _____ dwindles.

30. Read Hebrews 11:1.
    Faith produces evidence of our hope; but _____ is the springboard of our faith. Without _____, faith sputters and dies.

31. Others observe us from a _____ viewpoint; they lack a complete understanding of our devastations.

32. Hope must be _____.

33. Without hope, faith has nothing to which it can _____ itself. (Hope is the Velcro which fastens our faith.)

34. It is time to focus our expectations on _____.

35. Read Psalm 62:5-8.
    David knew that _____ but God could meet his expectations.

36. David knew that mere man could neither _____ nor save him.

37. Go back to your _____ love.

38. Go back to the place you knew the Lord in _____.

39. Many things might have changed in your life, but you still have _____.

40. The fact that you are here right now is the promise of _____ hope.

41. Now, shift the _____ back to Him.

42. _____ to the place of refuge and safety in Him.

Trust in Him at all times; ye people, pour out your heart before Him: God is a refuge for us. Selah (Psalm 62:8).

Digging Deeper Into Hope—

Read and discuss the Hope Quote at the beginning of this chapter of the Study Guide. Have you ever leaned on something or someone who failed you? Have you ever been at the point that you felt there was no way to recover hope? What did you do?

_____

_____

_____

_____

_____

_____

_____

_____

Hope in Action—

Repeat aloud 96 times the Hope Quote at the beginning of this chapter.
(FYI—That is once every 15 minutes around the clock!)

_____

_____

_____

CHAPTER FIVE

Out-of-Control Situations

"Whatever it may be that you have lost or feel that you have lost, God has not lost anything."

1. Read First Samuel 30:1-6.

   One of the most powerful stories of overcoming severe tragedy can be found in the Old Testament story of _____ at _____.

2. It was the _____ day of David's life.

3. In First Samuel 30:4, the Bible says that David _____ until he had no more power to weep.

4. There is a point of _____ that we all face at some Ziklag experience.

5. It was at this point of turning, that David made a _____ that would be talked about to this present day.

6. What was that destiny decision?

7. Read and memorize First Samuel 30:6. What are some of the possible ways that David might have encouraged himself in the Lord?

   a) _____

   b) _____

   c) _____

8. Read First Samuel 30:7-8.

   God told David that he would win and that he would _____ all.

   God is with us, even when we don't sense His nearness.

   ✐.

9. Write out Isaiah 43:2.

   _____

   _____

   _____

   _____

10. Read the first chapter of Job.

    In spite of Job's _____ to God, and perhaps even because of it, his life became the object of attack.

11. Sometimes the enemy tells us that the _____ we get to _____, the more bombardment is going to come our way.

12. This _____ enemy never tells us that the greater the conflict, the greater the _____.

13. Write out Job 3:25.

   _____

   _____

   _____

   _____

14. _____ is a common cause of loss.

15. _____ fear.

16. In its place, develop the _____ of God's love for you and His _____ for your life.

17. Read Philippians 4:8.
   Allow good _____ to fill your thought process.

18. After the trials of Job, he lived another _____ years and _____ the perpetual blessings of the Lord upon his life.

19. Read Job 42:10.
   The _____ _____ of Job was _____ _____ than his beginning.

20. In the end, you will see that your trials only served to
_____ you.

> *And the Lord turned the captivity of Job, when*
> *he prayed for his friends: also the Lord gave Job*
> *twice as much as he had before*
> # (Job 42:10).

Digging Deeper Into Hope—

Read and discuss the Hope Quote at the beginning of this chapter of the Study Guide. Have you ever been overwhelmed by loss? What kind of losses? How did you stay strong emotionally?

_____

_____

_____

_____

_____

Hope in Action—

Find a passage in the Book of Psalms and meditate throughout the day and evening upon God's faithfulness and strength.

_____

_____

CHAPTER SIX

This Is Not the Way to Live

"His grace, His life, His death, His resurrection were all gifts to me and to my life. No trial will ever change that."

1. _____ in the trial can become a captivating _____.

2. Satan loves to attack the _____ of your heavenly Father.

3. Read Luke 22:31-32 (KJV).

   In your own words, what did Jesus mean when He told Peter that He had prayed for him, *"that [his] faith fail not"*?

   _____

   _____

   _____

_____

_____

4. The strength of my position is always _____ _____.

5. This "in Christ" position is not based on our faith formulas, or our _____ on adversity.

6. It is a _____ position.

7. When hope is carved out of our lives by the sharp blades of calamity, our enemy begins to work at destroying our access to _____ _____.

8. Read John 10:1-30.
   Explain the difference between a thief and a robber.

   _____

   _____

   _____

   _____

9. This is the work of satan. He not only steals, but he _____, he trespasses, and he uses force and violence.

*No moments or lifetimes of adversity could
change what He did for me.*

10. The dictionary defines threaten as:

_____

_____

_____

_____

11. When the enemy strikes with his robbery and intimidation, he will threaten you, telling you that all your _____ are _____ forever and that you can never _____ or rebuild from the losses and brokenness.

> *The seeds of life, the seeds of hope, the seeds of promise, the seeds of potential, the seeds of destiny have all been planted into the believer at the new birth.*

12. The battle right now is over the _____ of the Word of God in your life!

13. Mark chapter _____ of the New Testament gives us the parable of the sower and the seed.

14. The seed gets _____.

    The seed _____.

    The seed _____.

    The seed _____.

15. This is the _____ of _____ that has been sown into your heart when you became a Christian.

16. Read Mark 4:15.
    Satan always comes to steal the _____ that has been sown into our lives.

17. God's Word is _____-_____.

18. His Word is _____.

19. When everything else is _____, God's Word still stands.

20. Write out Hebrews 4:12.

    _____

    _____

    _____

    _____

21. God's Word has the _____ and _____ to work in you, even when you feel that all _____ is lost.

22. It is not time to _____.

23. Read Psalm 119:16.
    Don't forget _____ _____, even when the sadness is all-consuming and life is _____.

24. Read Proverbs 30:5 in the Amplified Bible.
    This is the very moment that you need the Word of God to be your

    _____.

25. Read Second Timothy 3:16 in the Amplified Bible.

    At this moment, it is possible that the only _____ you have is that which comes forth from the _____ of God.

26. God's Word will produce an _____ in your life.

27. Read Genesis 3:1.

    One of the enemy's first modes of operation is to _____ _____ on the Word of God.

28. Your emotional erosion or ongoing emotional health will always be attached to your _____.

29. Your _____, as a believer, is in direct connection to the _____ of God that is _____ in your life.

30. If your _____ are focused on the Word, your emotions and life will reflect that.

31. The Word of God determines the way you _____.

32. The way you think determines the way you_____.

33. The way you feel determines the _____ you _____.

34. The way you act determines the _____ you form in life.

35. Your habits in life become your _____.

36. Your character will shape you for your _____.

37. Satan knows that your _____ is the only way that he can set up a _____. That is his method to destroy your life and annihilate your purpose.

38. A stronghold is a _____

_____.

39. This is why his first line of attack is against the _____ of God's nature, character, and Word.

40. Cumulative trials have a way of chipping away our tender _____ in God.

41. When our hope is gone, _____ has nothing to stick to.

42. There are no hopeless situations; only people who _____ hopeless in their situations.

43. It might seem hopeless to you, but not to _____.

44. _____ is going to see you through your situation.

45. God is going to make this test a _____.

The seeds of life, the seeds of hope, the seeds of promise, the seeds of potential, the seeds of destiny have all been planted into the believer at the new birth.

Digging Deeper Into Hope—

Read and discuss the Hope Quote at the beginning of this chapter of the Study Guide. Have you ever pondered the many things about God that are absolutely unchangeable gifts to your life? What are some of these gifts from the Lord?

_____

_____

_____

_____

_____

_____

_____

_____

Hope in Action—

List five gifts of the Lord that no trial will ever change.

_____

_____

_____

_____

_____

CHAPTER SEVEN

Turning Hopeless Situations Around

"There is no situation in your life too difficult for God to turn around."

1. All things are still _____ for the person who will take a stand in the Word of God.

2. Write out John 14:1.

   _____

   _____

   _____

3. You never have to overcome God's _____; you simply have to know how to lay hold of His _____.

4. Write out and memorize Hebrews 13:8.

   _____

_____

_____

_____

5. Jesus has already been in your _____.

6. He is in your _____.

7. He has already walked through your _____.

8. Hope's foundation is the _____ of _____.

9. Hope will produce a _____ _____ effect.

10. Read Isaiah 38:1-5.

    Hezekiah, a king in the Old Testament, was in what looked like a _____ situation.

11. King Hezekiah was not a perfect man, but he had a _____ that was turned toward God.

12. Hezekiah had been given a _____ _____.

13. But just when his situation looked hopeless, he turned his face toward the wall and started _____ _____.

14. What does it mean to "turn your face toward the wall"?

    _____

    _____

    _____

    _____

15. Write out Hebrews 12:2 from the Amplified Bible.

    _____

    _____

    _____

16. He (Hezekiah) looked away from every _____ until all he
    could see was _____.

17. Sometimes things happen in our lives and we are forced into a place
    where nothing but God gets our _____.

    Hezekiah showed God his tears. He fully
    revealed his heart to the Lord.

18. Go before God and God alone, and tell Him the _____ of
    your _____.

19. Read First Samuel 16:7.
    God looks on the _____.

20. Even when you have _____, _____ the mark, or _____,
    God still looks at your _____ and intentions.

21. Read First John 1:9.
    God is not holding your _____ against you.

22. Read Micah 7:19.
    Once you _____, God forgets about your sins.

23. Don't bring up something God has chosen to _____.

24. Don't allow your _____ to stop you from moving into your

    _____.

25. Your _____ cannot stop God from turning a hopeless perspective around!

26. Read Matthew 7:1-5.

    Don't judge others because of their _____.

27. Endings are a time of new _____.

28. Confess: "This is the _____ of what I have been going through. God has a new _____ for me now."

29. Build your _____ for your new beginning.

30. Don't let anyone else's _____ of you form your reality.

31. _____ will return to your life as you begin to build your confidence of who you are in Christ Jesus.

32. Your self-worth, self-esteem, and self-value already have been determined in _____ _____.

33. Get back to this basic _____ _____ of life.

34. Read Judges 6:12.

    Gideon, in the Old Testament, had a very poor _____ of himself.

35. He was filled with _____ and _____.

36. But an Angel came to Gideon and called him a _____ _____ of valor.

37. You might see yourself one way, but _____ _____ you another.

38. Don't set your opinions in stone until you consult God's _____.

39. Ask God to reveal your immeasurable _____.

40. Ask Him for _____ to walk in His Word and in His estimation of your life.

41. Pursue the _____ that God has placed before you.

42. _____ _____ are better than no steps at all!

43. Look through the lens of the _____ of God and the vision of the _____ _____ for your life.

44. In taking the time to rebuild your confidence, you will have many opportunities to be stretched in the area of _____.

45. Name four ways to boost your endurance.

    a) _____

    b) _____

    c) _____

    d) _____

46. Write out and memorize Romans 8:31.

_____

_____

_____

_____

47. Never doubt who _____is.

48. Never doubt your ability to be _____ in Christ.

49. Open your mouth and _____ the Word of God over your life.

Don't let self-doubt rob you. Refuse to be undermined by belittling thoughts about yourself.

Digging Deeper Into Hope—

Read and discuss the Hope Quote at the beginning of this chapter of the Study Guide. Think about, and discuss, some of the miracles in the Bible. Does God specialize in the impossible? Explain.

_____

_____

_____

_____

_____

_____

Hope in Action—

Today, invest some time praying for endurance during your time of testing.

_____

_____

_____

_____

CHAPTER EIGHT

Lost Hope Restored

"God has called you to your now and to your future."

1. Read Acts 27.

   The _____ is full of real-life stories of people, just like you, whose _____ and _____ were dashed to the ground.

2. One of these people was the apostle _____.

3. While he and others were on board the ship, a _____ arose.

4. There could be death in this wind and there certainly would be _____.

5. Sometimes in order to take us higher, certain things have to _____ in our lives.

6. We have to leave the concerns that we don't understand, recognize, know, and comprehend in the _____ of the Lord.

7. Maybe there are things we thought we could never live without or do without. Then, suddenly, we find ourselves in a place where these_____, _____ or _____ or even _____ are somehow gone from our lives.

8. The letting go…is all a part of our _____ to our _____, who alone is able to make all _____ abound regardless of the situation. (Read Second Corinthians 9:8 AMP.)

9. We are _____, not owners, of what God allows us to have.

10. What is a steward? _____

11. Read Psalm 24:1.
_____ is the Master, Owner, and Possessor of all things.

12. _____ was an experienced seaman, having had many journeys by treacherous waters.

13. Read Second Corinthians 11:23-30.
This man was _____ to storms, hardships, difficulties, adversities, and suffering.

14. However, as a prisoner on board this particular sailing vessel in Acts 27, all _____ was gone.

15. Paul had _____ direction during disaster.

16. Read Acts 27:20.

    For Paul and all on board, there was _____ sense of _____ once the sun and stars were hidden.

> *Now the God of hope fill you with all joy and peace in believing, that ye may abound in hope, through the power of the Holy Ghost* (Romans 15:13).

17. Even here, God has still promised to _____ us.

18. Your storm never stops the general direction of the _____ of God.

19. You can still move _____ your victory, your wholeness, your destiny, His plan, His purposes.

20. You do not have to wait until you _____ ____ _____ _____ for God to move for you or use you.

21. Read Luke 10:30-37.

    The _____ _____ poured in the oil and the wine right there on the Jericho road and then he put the wounded man on his own beast.

22. He did not wait until things got _____.

23. He did something _____ _____ and there.

24. Read Psalm 119:105-106 (AMP).

    God's promise to guide you has not been _____ by your

    _____.

25. Your _____ days can still produce something for Him.

26. Paul began to _____ hope through prayer.

27. What is an incubator? _____

    _____

    _____

    _____

28. Paul went to this incubator called _____ and God brought

    _____ into a hopeless circumstance.

29. Jesus is our Healer. He is the balm for our _____ lives.

30. He is our Great Physician. He can _____ your _____ heart

    and life.

31. He is the _____ of broken-down lives.

32. Read First Timothy 1:1.

    Jesus is still _____ _____.

33. Not only did Paul make it through alive, but everyone on board was

    _____.

34. Then Paul ministered on the island of _____ in the very spot

    where the storm had so mercilessly spit them out.

35. This place that could have been their _____ became their place of _____.

36. A strong center of Christianity was established on the island as a _____ of the _____.

37. Write out and memorize Romans 8:28.

    _____

    _____

    _____

38. Your _____ can work for your good and for God's glory.

39. Read Genesis 37; 39; 40-41.

    _____ was a dreamer.

*There is a plan that God is working, even when
we do not see Him at work.*

40. Joseph's story is one of extreme _____ and suspense, heartache and _____.

41. You must be _____ with your pain if you are going to be honest with your _____.

42. If you _____ the pain, you will _____ the recovery.

43. God wants you _____ whole.

44. Your _____ is vital to your effectiveness and enjoyment of life.

45. No _____ has the power to destroy you.

46. We learn to _____ God in the hardest of times.

47. We trust that _____ _____ what is best and that whatever it takes for Him to work that out, He will do it.

48. Young Joseph went through setup after setup that put him in positions where he had to _____ on God.

49. What is one of the primary lessons that we learn from the life of Joseph? _____

_____

_____

_____

50. In the house of Potiphar, Joseph would quickly advance because of his heart of _____ and his excellent _____.

51. He had no way of knowing that he was in for another _____ of his dream that would put him in a different kind of pit called *prison*.

52. Sleeping, for many years, on a mat more than likely stained with blood, urine, feces, and vomit, Joseph would once again find _____.

53. Little did he know that he was about to get off of life's floor
    _____.

54. Joseph was imprisoned for a crime he did not commit, but God had
    not _____ him.

55. For all you know, the very thing you thought would kill you, might
    actually position you for greater _____.

56. All of the adversities of life had served to _____ Joseph for the
    fulfillment of the dreams God had given him.

57. Let Joseph's story give you _____.

58. You do not have to live an _____ life; you can live the
    abundant life Christ has already provided.

59. Just as Joseph was released from prison after an "overnight" stay of
    13 years, in one day, your life can be changed from _____ to
    ever-increasing _____.

60. Joseph was _____even when he didn't know it.

61. He was favored even when _____ _____ of his life
    _____God's manifested favor.

62. You are _____ even when you don't feel like it.

63. You are _____ when others say you are not.

64. No one can decide the ultimate _____ of _____ for your life.

65. God's _____ abounds where sins, shortcomings, mishaps, and confusions abound.

66. Read Hebrews 4:16 AMP.

    God's grace abounds where _____ exists.

67. Let me encourage you that _____ cannot destroy you.

68. They will _____, _____, and _____ you, but they cannot _____ you.

69. The measure of your success in life is related directly to your ability to handle _____.

70. Define disappointment. _____

    _____

    _____

    _____

71. Joseph's dreams had been _____ over and over again.

72. God had _____ Joseph in the most complex of

    _____.

73. He had thoroughly sent His chosen servant through the rigors of _____ toughness and _____ to survive the hardest of times.

74. Joseph was ready for such an _____.

75. All of life's disappointments, all of the heartache and betrayal, all of the loneliness and misunderstandings, were about to be

_____.

76. Read Genesis 50:20.

His brothers meant it all for evil, but God meant it for

_____.

77. God has a _____ for your life that will go beyond anything that you can ever dream or _____.

78. _____ is not your destiny.

79. Read Ephesians 3:20 (AMP).

In fact, you have just been positioned to _____ again.

80. Write out at least two of the hope statements relating to purpose.

_____

_____

_____

_____

81. God has a plan for your life and the _____ _____ will not rest until it is fulfilled.

82. Give three characteristics of the Holy Spirit as they pertain to the purposes of God in your life.

a) _____

b) _____

c) _____

83. Your whole _____ has been an education in who God really meant for you to be.

84. It is not just about the destination, but about what happens _____ of us along the way.

85. Purpose is intrinsically linked to _____.

86. The Holy Spirit turns victims into _____.

87. A strong life is not just wishes and intentions but purpose and peak _____ within that purpose.

88. You have to _____ for your purpose in life.

89. _____ is such a precious gift.

90. Now that we have survived and now that we have come through the worst storms of our lives, we are ready to pour sacrificially and generously into God's _____ purpose for our lives.

91. Deep down in your heart and soul, you are now ready to tap into God's magnanimous _____ of _____ and dispense it unreservedly to _____.

92. Each day holds new _____ to explore God's purpose without _____.

93. The _____ of your life is the _____ of your life!

Sometimes we just have to slow down, get all of the extra static out of our lives and listen to our hearts.

Digging Deeper Into Hope—

Read and discuss the Hope Quote at the beginning of this chapter of the Study Guide. Having read the Scriptures in this book, do you now know that God has a plan for your life, regardless of the battles you have faced? Do you believe that you are now on your way to greater hope in Him? Explain.

_____

_____

_____

_____

_____

_____

_____

_____

_____

Hope in Action—

Invest one hour in praise and worship to God for the glorious things He has planned for your life!

_____

_____

_____

_____

_____

Hope in His Word

John 16:33 AMP

I have told you these things, so that in Me you may have [perfect] peace and confidence. In the world you have tribulation and trials and distress and frustration; but be of good cheer [take courage; be confident, certain, undaunted]! For I have overcome the world. [I have deprived it of power to harm you and have conquered it for you.]

Isaiah 61:3 NKJV

…To give them beauty for ashes, the oil of joy for mourning, the garment of praise for the spirit of heaviness…

Psalm 145:14 NKJV

The Lord upholds all who fall, and raises up all who are bowed down.

Psalm 34:18 NKJV

The Lord is near to those who have a broken heart, and saves such as have a contrite spirit.

John 10:10 NKJV

...I have come that they may have life, and that they may have it more abundantly.

Deuteronomy 33:27 KJV

The eternal God is thy refuge, and underneath are the everlasting arms: and He shall thrust out the enemy from before thee; and shall say, Destroy them.

Psalm 23:4 KJV

Yea, though I walk through the valley of the shadow of death, I will fear no evil: for Thou art with me; Thy rod and Thy staff they comfort me.

Proverbs 12:25 MSG

Worry weighs us down; a cheerful word picks us up.

Proverbs 15:4 MSG

Kind words heal and help; cutting words wound and maim.

Isaiah 50:4 AMP

[The Servant of God says] The Lord God has given Me the tongue of a disciple and of one who is taught, that I should know how to

speak a word in season to him who is weary. He wakens Me morning by morning, He wakens My ear to hear as a disciple [as one who is taught].

Matthew 5:4 MSG

You're blessed when you feel you've lost what is most dear to you. Only then can you be embraced by the One most dear to you.

John 14:18 AMP

I will not leave you as orphans [comfortless, desolate, bereaved, forlorn, helpless]; I will come [back] to you.

2 Thessalonians 2:16-17 AMP

Now may our Lord Jesus Christ Himself and God our Father, Who loved us and gave us everlasting consolation and encouragement and well-founded hope through [His] grace (unmerited favor), comfort and encourage your hearts and strengthen them [make them steadfast and keep them unswerving] in every good work and word.

Isaiah 40:31 KJV

But they that wait upon the Lord shall renew their strength; they shall mount up with wings as eagles; they shall run, and not be weary; [and] they shall walk, and not faint.

2 Corinthians 1:4 KJV

Who comforteth us in all our tribulation, that we may be able to comfort them which are in any trouble, by the comfort wherewith we ourselves are comforted of God.

2 Chronicles 16:9 NASB

For the eyes of the Lord move to and fro throughout the earth that He may strongly support those whose heart is completely His.

Proverbs 11:2 AMP

When swelling and pride come, then emptiness and shame come also, but with the humble (those who are lowly, who have been pruned or chiseled by trial, and renounce self) are skillful and godly Wisdom and soundness.

Isaiah 55:10-11 AMP

For as the rain and snow come down from the heavens, and return not there again, but water the earth and make it bring forth and sprout, that it may give seed to the sower and bread to the eater, so shall My word be that goes forth out of My mouth: it shall not return to Me void [without producing any effect, useless], but it shall accomplish that which I please and purpose, and it shall prosper in the thing for which I sent it.

Joshua 1:9 NIV

Have I not commanded you? Be strong and courageous. Do not be terrified; do not be discouraged, for the Lord your God will be with you wherever you go.

Micah 7:7 AMP

But as for me, I will look to the Lord and confident in Him I will keep watch; I will wait with hope and expectancy for the God of my salvation; my God will hear me.

Hebrews 10:35 AMP

Do not, therefore, fling away your fearless confidence, for it carries a great and glorious compensation of reward.

Psalm 107: 8-9 KJV

Oh that men would praise the Lord for His goodness, and for His wonderful works to the children of men! For He satisfieth the longing soul, and filleth the hungry soul with goodness.

Deuteronomy 31:6 KJV

Be strong and of a good courage, fear not, nor be afraid of them: for the Lord thy God, He it is that doth go with thee; He will not fail thee, nor forsake thee.

Psalm 27:14 KJV

Wait on the Lord: be of good courage, and He shall strengthen thine heart: wait, I say, on the Lord.

1 John 5:14 AMP

And this is the confidence (the assurance, the privilege of boldness) which we have in Him: [we are sure] that if we ask anything (make any request) according to His will (in agreement with His own plan), He listens to and hears us.

Psalm 3:3 NLT

But You, O Lord, are a shield around me; You are my glory, the one who holds my head high.

Colossians 3:2 AMP

And set your minds and keep them set on what is above (the higher things), not on the things that are on the earth.

Isaiah 40:31 AMP

But those who wait for the Lord [who expect, look for, and hope in Him] shall change and renew their strength and power; they shall lift their wings and mount up [close to God] as eagles [mount up to the sun]; they shall run and not be weary, they shall walk and not faint or become tired.

Isaiah 60:1 AMP

Arise [from the depression and prostration in which circumstances have kept you—rise to a new life]! Shine (be radiant with the glory of the Lord), for your light has come, and the glory of the Lord has risen upon you!

1 Peter 5:9 AMP

Withstand him; be firm in faith [against his onset—rooted, established, strong, immovable, and determined], knowing that the same (identical) sufferings are appointed to your brotherhood (the whole body of Christians) throughout the world.

Proverbs 8:17 KJV

I love them that love Me; and those that seek Me early shall find Me.

2 Corinthians 4:8-9 KJV

We are troubled on every side, yet not distressed; we are perplexed, but not in despair; persecuted, but not forsaken; cast down, but not destroyed…

2 Corinthians 12:9 AMP

But He said to me, My grace (My favor and loving-kindness and mercy) is enough for you [sufficient against any danger and enables you to bear the trouble manfully]; for My strength and power are made perfect (fulfilled and completed) and show themselves most effective in [your] weakness. Therefore, I will all the more gladly glory in my weaknesses and infirmities, that the strength and power of Christ (the Messiah) may rest (yes, may pitch a tent over and dwell) upon me!

Psalm 34:18 MSG

If your heart is broken, you'll find God right there; if you're kicked in the gut, He'll help you catch your breath.

Psalm 42:5 AMP

Why are you cast down, O my inner self? And why should you moan over me and be disquieted within me? Hope in God and wait expectantly for Him, for I shall yet praise Him, my Help and my God.

Psalm 27:5 KJV

For in the time of trouble He shall hide me in His pavilion: in the secret of His tabernacle shall He hide me; He shall set me up upon a rock.

Psalm 31:7 NLT

I will be glad and rejoice in your unfailing love, for you have seen my troubles, and you care about the anguish of my soul.

Psalm 57:1-3 MSG

Be good to me, God—and now! I've run to You for dear life. I'm hiding out under Your wings until the hurricane blows over. I call out to High God, the God who holds me together. He sends orders from heaven and saves me, He humiliates those who kick me around. God delivers generous love, He makes good on His word.

Psalm 119:50 AMP

This is my comfort and consolation in my affliction: that Your word has revived me and given me life.

2 Corinthians 4:17-18 AMP

For our light, momentary affliction (this slight distress of the passing hour) is ever more and more abundantly preparing and producing and achieving for us an everlasting weight of glory [beyond all measure, excessively surpassing all comparisons and all calculations, a vast and transcendent glory and blessedness never to cease!], since we consider and look not to the things that are seen but to the things that are unseen; for the things that are visible are temporal (brief and fleeting), but the things that are invisible are deathless and everlasting.

Romans 10:17 KJV

So then faith cometh by hearing, and hearing by the word of God.

Romans 5:20 KJV

…But where sin abounded, grace did much more abound…

Romans 15:13 AMP

May the God of your hope so fill you with all joy and peace in believing [through the experience of your faith] that by the power of the Holy Spirit you may abound and be overflowing (bubbling over) with hope.

2 Corinthians 5:7 KJV

…We walk by faith, not by sight…

Hebrews 11:1 KJV

Now faith is the substance of things hoped for, the evidence of things not seen.

Hebrews 11:6 KJV

But without faith it is impossible to please Him: for he that cometh to God must believe that He is, and that He is a rewarder of them that diligently seek Him.

2 Timothy 1:7 AMP

For God did not give us a spirit of timidity (of cowardice, of craven and cringing and fawning fear), but [He has given us a spirit] of power and of love and of calm and well-balanced mind and discipline and self-control.

Matthew 6:14 AMP

For if you forgive people their trespasses [their reckless and willful sins, leaving them, letting them go, and giving up resentment], your heavenly Father will also forgive you.

Colossians 3:13 NLT

Make allowance for each other's faults, and forgive anyone who offends you. Remember, the Lord forgave you, so you must forgive others.

James 5:15 MSG

Believing-prayer will heal you, and Jesus will put you on your feet. And if you've sinned, you'll be forgiven—healed inside and out.

Isaiah 53:5 AMP

But He was wounded for our transgressions, He was bruised for our guilt and iniquities; the chastisement [needful to obtain] peace and well-being for us was upon Him, and with the stripes [that wounded] Him we are healed and made whole.

Psalm 107:20 AMP

He sends forth His word and heals them and rescues them from the pit and destruction.

Isaiah 58:8 AMP

Then shall your light break forth like the morning, and your healing (your restoration and the power of a new life) shall spring forth speedily; your righteousness (your rightness, your justice, and your right relationship with God) shall go before you [conducting you to peace and prosperity], and the glory of the Lord shall be your rear guard.

Deuteronomy 28:1 AMP

If you will listen diligently to the voice of the Lord your God, being watchful to do all His commandments which I command you this day, the Lord your God will set you high above all the nations of the earth.

Jeremiah 29:11 AMP

For I know the thoughts and plans that I have for you, says the Lord, thoughts and plans for welfare and peace and not for evil, to give you hope in your final outcome.

Romans 12:1-2 MSG

So here's what I want you to do, God helping you: Take your everyday, ordinary life—your sleeping, eating, going-to-work, and walking-around life—and place it before God as an offering.

Embracing what God does for you is the best thing you can do for Him. Don't become so well-adjusted to your culture that you fit into it without even thinking. Instead, fix your attention on God. You'll be changed from the inside out. Readily recognize what He wants from you, and quickly respond to it. Unlike the culture around you, always dragging you down to its level of immaturity, God brings the best out of you, develops well-formed maturity in you.

Psalm 33:18 AMP

Behold, the Lord's eye is upon those who fear Him [who revere and worship Him with awe], who wait for Him and hope in His mercy and loving-kindness…

1 Corinthians 6:19-20 AMP

Do you not know that your body is the temple (the very sanctuary) of the Holy Spirit Who lives within you, Whom you have received [as a Gift] from God? You are not your own, you were bought with a price [purchased with a preciousness and paid for, made His own]. So then, honor God and bring glory to Him in your body.

1 John 1:9 AMP

If we [freely] admit that we have sinned and confess our sins, He is faithful and just (true to His own nature and promises) and will forgive our sins [dismiss our lawlessness] and [continuously] cleanse us from all unrighteousness [everything not in conformity to His will in purpose, thought, and action].

Proverbs 13:12 KJV

Hope deferred maketh the heart sick: but when the desire cometh, it is a tree of life.

1 Corinthians 13:13 MSG

But for right now, until that completeness, we have three things to do to lead us toward that consummation: Trust steadily in God, hope unswervingly, love extravagantly. And the best of the three is love.

Romans 8:37 AMP

Yet amid all these things we are more than conquerors and gain a surpassing victory through Him Who loved us.

Lamentations 3:24-26 AMP

The Lord is my portion or share, says my living being (my inner self); therefore will I hope in Him and wait expectantly for Him. The Lord is good to those who wait hopefully and expectantly for Him, to those who seek Him [inquire of and for Him and require Him by right of necessity and on the authority of God's word]. It is good that one should hope in and wait quietly for the salvation (the safety and ease) of the Lord.

James 4:10 AMP

Humble yourselves [feeling very insignificant] in the presence of the Lord, and He will exalt you [He will lift you up and make your lives significant].

1 Peter 5:6 KJV

Humble yourselves therefore under the mighty hand of God, that He may exalt you in due time…

Psalm 91:1 AMP

He who dwells in the secret place of the Most High shall remain stable and fixed under the shadow of the Almighty [Whose power no foe can withstand].

1 John 4:4 KJV

Ye are of God, little children, and have overcome them: because greater is He that is in you, than he that is in the world.

2 Corinthians 12:9 NLT

Each time He said, "My grace is all you need. My power works best in weakness." So now I am glad to boast about my weaknesses, so that the power of Christ can work through me.

Philippians 4:13 AMP

I have strength for all things in Christ Who empowers me [I am ready for anything and equal to anything through Him Who infuses inner strength into me; I am self-sufficient in Christ's sufficiency].

Psalm 25:21 MSG

Use all Your skill to put me together; I wait to see Your finished product.

Proverbs 20:4 NLT

Those too lazy to plow in the right season will have no food at the harvest.

Hebrews 6:11-12 KJV

And we desire that every one of you do shew the same diligence to the full assurance of hope unto the end: that ye be not slothful, but followers of them who through faith and patience inherit the promises.

Psalm 46:1 KJV

God is our refuge and strength, a very present help in trouble.

Psalm 40:1 AMP

I waited patiently and expectantly for the Lord; and He inclined to me and heard my cry.

Ecclesiastes 7:8 KJV

Better is the end of a thing than the beginning thereof: and the patient in spirit is better than the proud in spirit.

Job 22:21 AMP

Acquaint now yourself with Him [agree with God and show yourself to be conformed to His will] and be at peace; by that [you shall prosper and great] good shall come to you.

Isaiah 26:3 AMP

You will guard him and keep him in perfect and constant peace whose mind [both its inclination and its character] is stayed on You, because he commits himself to You, leans on You, and hopes confidently in You.

Philippians 4:7 AMP

And God's peace [shall be yours, that tranquil state of a soul assured of its salvation through Christ, and so fearing nothing from God and being content with its earthly lot of whatever sort that is, that peace] which transcends all understanding shall garrison and mount guard over your hearts and minds in Christ Jesus.

Isaiah 40:29 KJV

He giveth power to the faint; and to them that have no might He increaseth strength.

Luke 10:19 AMP

Behold! I have given you authority and power to trample upon serpents and scorpions, and [physical and mental strength and ability] over all the power that the enemy [possesses]; and nothing shall in any way harm you.

Acts 1:8 AMP

But you shall receive power (ability, efficiency, and might) when the Holy Spirit has come upon you, and you shall be My witnesses in Jerusalem and all Judea and Samaria and to the ends (the very bounds) of the earth.

Ephesians 3:16 AMP

May He grant you out of the rich treasury of His glory to be strengthened and reinforced with mighty power in the inner man by the [Holy] Spirit [Himself indwelling your innermost being and personality].

Job 22:27 KJV

Thou shalt make thy prayer unto Him, and He shall hear thee, and thou shalt pay thy vows.

Isaiah 55:6 KJV

Seek ye the Lord while He may be found, call ye upon Him while He is near...

Matthew 7:7 KJV

Ask, and it shall be given you; seek, and ye shall find; knock, and it shall be opened unto you...

Matthew 18:19 AMP

Again I tell you, if two of you on earth agree (harmonize together, make a symphony together) about whatever [anything and everything] they may ask, it will come to pass and be done for them by My Father in heaven.

Luke 18:1 AMP

Also [Jesus] told them a parable to the effect that they ought always to pray and not to turn coward (faint, lose heart, and give up).

Romans 8:26 AMP

So too the [Holy] Spirit comes to our aid and bears us up in our weakness; for we do not know what prayer to offer nor how to offer it worthily as we ought, but the Spirit Himself goes to meet our supplication and pleads in our behalf with unspeakable yearnings and groanings too deep for utterance.

Hebrews 4:16 AMP

Let us then fearlessly and confidently and boldly draw near to the throne of grace (the throne of God's unmerited favor to us sinners), that we may receive mercy [for our failures] and find grace to help in good time for every need [appropriate help and well-timed help, coming just when we need it].

1 Peter 4:12-13 MSG

Friends, when life gets really difficult, don't jump to the conclusion that God isn't on the job. Instead, be glad that you are in the very thick of what Christ experienced. This is a spiritual refining process, with glory just around the corner.

Philippians 4:19 KJV

But my God shall supply all your need according to His riches in glory by Christ Jesus.

Job 23:10 AMP

But He knows the way that I take [He has concern for it, appreciates, and pays attention to it]. When He has tried me, I shall come forth as refined gold [pure and luminous].

Romans 5:5 KJV

And hope maketh not ashamed; because the love of God is shed abroad in our hearts by the Holy Ghost which is given unto us.

Jude 20-21 AMP

But you, beloved, build yourselves up [founded] on your most holy faith [make progress, rise like an edifice higher and higher], praying in the Holy Spirit; guard and keep yourselves in the love of God; expect and patiently wait for the mercy of our Lord Jesus Christ (the Messiah)—[which will bring you] unto life eternal.

Romans 8:31 KJV

What shall we then say to these things? If God be for us, who can be against us?

Psalm 37:5 AMP

Commit your way to the Lord [roll and repose each care of your load on Him]; trust (lean on, rely on, and be confident) also in Him and He will bring it to pass.

2 Chronicles 7:14 KJV

If My people, which are called by My name, shall humble themselves, and pray, and seek My face, and turn from their wicked ways; then will I hear from heaven, and will forgive their sin, and will heal their land.

Matthew 6:33 AMP

But seek (aim at and strive after) first of all His kingdom and His righteousness (His way of doing and being right), and then all these things taken together will be given you besides.

Ephesians 6:11 AMP

Put on God's whole armor [the armor of a heavy-armed soldier which God supplies], that you may be able successfully to stand up against [all] the strategies and the deceits of the devil.

Isaiah 40:29 KJV

He giveth power to the faint; and to them that have no might He increaseth strength.

1 Peter 5:7 AMP

Casting the whole of your care [all your anxieties, all your worries, all your concerns, once and for all] on Him, for He cares for you affectionately and cares about you watchfully.

Jeremiah 30:17 KJV

For I will restore health unto thee, and I will heal thee of thy wounds, saith the Lord…

James 4:7-10 MSG

So let God work His will in you. Yell a loud no to the Devil and watch him scamper. Say a quiet yes to God and He'll be there in no time. Quit dabbling in sin. Purify your inner life. Quit playing the field. Hit bottom, and cry your eyes out. The fun and games are over. Get serious, really serious. Get down on your knees before the Master; it's the only way you'll get on your feet.

Proverbs 18:9 AMP

He who is loose and slack in his work is brother to him who is a destroyer and he who does not use his endeavors to heal himself is brother to him who commits suicide.

Proverbs 18:21 KJV

Death and life are in the power of the tongue: and they that love it shall eat the fruit thereof.

Psalm 62:8 AMP

Trust in, lean on, rely on, and have confidence in Him at all times, you people; pour out your hearts before Him. God is a refuge for us (a fortress and a high tower). Selah [pause, and calmly think of that]!

Romans 12:1 NIV

Therefore, I urge you, brothers, in view of God's mercy, to offer your bodies as living sacrifices, holy and pleasing to God—this is your spiritual act of worship.

Isaiah 30:18 AMP

And therefore the Lord [earnestly] waits [expecting, looking, and longing] to be gracious to you; and therefore He lifts Himself up, that He may have mercy on you and show loving-kindness to you. For the Lord is a God of justice. Blessed (happy, fortunate, to be envied) are all those who [earnestly] wait for Him, who expect and look and long for Him [for His victory, His favor, His love, His peace, His joy, and His matchless, unbroken companionship]!

James 1:5 KJV

If any of you lack wisdom, let him ask of God, that giveth to all men liberally, and upbraideth not; and it shall be given him.

John 4:24 KJV

God is a Spirit: and they that worship Him must worship Him in spirit and in truth.

Psalm 27:14 AMP

Wait and hope for and expect the Lord; be brave and of good courage and let your heart be stout and enduring. Yes, wait for and hope for and expect the Lord.

Answer Guide

Chapter 1:

1. a) exist b) real c) loves

2. Job

3. God Zone; tangible presence

4. say; know; lives

5. hope

6. prayer

7. Prayer

8. nurturing; womb; faith

9. Romans 15:13

10. no; prayer

11. breeding ground

12. talking; God

13. gushing; heart

14. Jesus; interceding

15. brokenness

16. grace

17. come between

18. a) to strike upon b) to assail

one with petitions c) to come between d) to urge

19. Intercession

20. a) become aggressive b) get on the offensive c) move God's plan from Heaven to earth

21. heart's

22. painful; calamities

23. cries; cry; cannot

24. before

25. faith; trust

Chapter 2:

1. 2 Corinthians 4:17

2. beginning

3. wilderness; passageway

4. cross

5. intelligence

6. stop

7. demonic; mind

8. God

9. declare; His agenda; blood; no

10. assignment

11. a) sin; rebellion b) lack; knowledge c) from this position; He wants

12. vision; person

13. adversity

14. designed; planned

15. deferred; delayed

16. hope; hope

17. not

18. flies

19. nature

20. a) carriers b) breed c) invade d) attracted

21. open wounds

22. junk; sins; attitudes

23. on fire

24. despair; hopelessness

25. Hopelessness

26. hope

27. purpose; Assignment

28. Romans 8:37

Chapter 3:

1. life; God; purposes; Kingdom

2. assignment

3. lane

4. quit

5. distracted; lane

6. oil

7. processed

8. myrrh

9. bitter

10. anointing oil

11. pressing

12. accelerate

13. pressed; formed

14. anointing

15. indicators

16. storms; building materials

17. build strength; endurance

18. pressure

19. foundation

20. rock

21. Christ Jesus

22. a) spiritually b) physically c) mentally d) relationally e) financially f) in your destiny

23. direction

24. prayer

25. Prayer

26. pray

27. perspective

28. why

29. positions your spirit

30. John 16:33

Chapter 4:

1. dreams

2. abilities

3. hope

4. Having Optimistic Positive Expectations

5. build; rebuild

6. years

7. restoring

8. Choose two Scriptures from the "in Christ" list.

9. patch you

10. new

11. deconstruction; reconstruction

12. Luke 4:18

13. broken down

14. beauty; ashes

15. hurting

16. emotional

17. compassion

18. mess; before

19. broken

20. barricaded

21. intention; decision

22. died

23. came

24. not over

25. situations; dead

26. perfect

27. expectations; hopes

28. Unmet; misplaced

29. hope

30. hope; hope

31. limited

32. restored

33. attach

34. God

35. nobody

36. deliver

37. first

38. pureness

39. God

40. renewed

41. focus

42. Run

Chapter 5:

1. David; Ziklag

2. worst

3. wept

4. breaking

5. decision

6. He encouraged himself in the Lord.

7. a) thought about how many

times God had spared his life up to that point b) praised God c) went into immediate prayer.

8. recover

9. Isaiah 43:2

10. devotion

11. closer; God

12. deceptive; victory

13. Job 3:25

14. Fear

15. Refuse

16. confidence; plan

17. expectations

18. enjoyed

19. latter end; more blessed

20. promote

Chapter 6:

1. Entrapment; mind-set

2. integrity

3. Get back to the most basic belief in which all of Christianity stands—Faith in Christ Jesus alone and His finished work—not faith formulas.

4. in Christ

5. perspectives

6. "gift"

7. God's ability

8. A thief takes goods; a robber enters with force or violence, intimidations and threat.

9. threatens

10. an expression of intention to inflict evil, injury or damage

11. hopes; lost; recover

12. integrity

13. 4

14. planted; overcomes; grows; multiplies

15. Word; God

16. Word

17. self-sufficient

18. settled

19. shaken

20. Hebrews 4:12

21. power; ability; hope

22. quit

23. God's Word; unbearable

24. refuge

25. breath; Word

26. effect

27. cast doubt

28. thinking

29. thinking; Word; active

30. thoughts

31. think

32. feel

33. decisions; make

34. habits

35. character

36. destiny

37. thinking; stronghold

38. demonic fortification established by wrong thinking

39. integrity

40. hopes

41. faith

42. feel

43. God

44. God

45. testimony

Chapter 7:

1. possible

2. John 14:1

3. reluctance; willingness

4. Hebrews 13:8

5. yesterdays

6. todays

7. tomorrows

8. Word; God

9. life-giving

10. hopeless

11. heart

12. death sentence

13. seeking God

14. turn away from everything else that is pulling you, distracting you, or taking your focus away from God and His plans for you

15. Hebrews 12:2 (AMP)

16. distraction; God

17. attention

18. thoughts; heart

19. heart

20. failed; missed; sinned; heart

21. sins

22. repent

23. forget

24. past; future

25. past

26. situation

27. beginnings

28. end; beginning

29. confidence

30. opinion

31. Stabilization

32. Christ Jesus

33. building block

34. opinion

35. doubt; fear

36. mighty man

37. God sees

38. opinions

39. value

40. strength

41. goals

42. Baby steps

43. Word; Holy Spirit

44. endurance

45. a) surround yourself with encouraging believers b) Lay aside every weight that you should not be carrying c) Get all the sin out of your heart and life d) Set your eyes on Jesus

46. Romans 8:31

47. God

48. productive

49. speak

Chapter 8:

1. Bible; hopes; dreams

2. Paul

3. storm

4. damage

5. shift

6. hands

7. places; things; people

8. surrender; God; grace

9. stewards

10. one who watches over things

that belong to someone else

11. God

12. Paul

13. accustomed

14. hope

15. no

16. no; direction

17. lead

18. move

19. toward

20. get it all together

21. good Samaritan

22. better

23. right then

24. voided; trials

25. darkest

26. incubate

27. a chamber used to provide

controlled environmental conditions…for…cultivation

28. prayer; hope

29. troubled

30. heal; broken

31. restorer

32. our hope

33. spared

34. Malta

35. death; provision

36. result; storm

37. Romans 8:28

38. storm

39. Joseph

40. emotion; restoration

41. honest; recovery

42. mask; mask

43. totally

44. wholeness

45. situation

46. trust

47. God knows

48. depend

49. Even when we are going through the most extreme trials, God has not forgotten about us. He is providentially working on our behalf, even when we are not aware of it.

50. integrity; servanthood

51. sabotage

52. favor

53. permanently

54. forgotten

55. effectiveness

56. position

57. hope

58. imitation

59. hopelessness; joy

60. favored

61. every situation; challenged

62. favored

63. favored

64. will; God

65. grace

66. need

67. disappointments

68. strengthen; intensify; temper; destroy

69. disappointment

70. the act or an instance of disappointing: the state or emotion of being disappointed; the act of disappointing, or the state of being disappointed; defeat or failure of expectation or hope; miscarriage of design or plan; frustration.

71. miscarried

72. prepared; environments

73. mental; skill

74. assignment

75. recompensed

76. good

77. plan; imagine

78. Quitting

79. hope

80. (Choose any two of the five hope statements relating to your purpose.)

81. Holy Spirit

82. a) aggressive b) passionate c) relentless

83. journey

84. inside

85. fulfillment

86. victors

87. performance

88. go

89. Life

90. Kingdom

91. reservoirs; hope; others

92. opportunities; limits

93. rest; best

Author Ministry Page

For the latest in news and ministry information from Jana Alcorn Ministries, please visit us online at:

www.JanaAlcorn.com

www.Facebook.com/JanaAlcorn

www.Twitter.com/JanaAlcorn

For latest updates on causes that promote HOPE, visit:

www.DreamChildFoundation.org

Contact Our Office:

Jana Alcorn Ministries

P.O. Box 4500

Huntsville, AL 35815

USA

Office phone: 256.470.0454

E-mail: info@JanaAlcorn.com

Other Books By Jana Alcorn

99 Keys of Hope

99 Keys of Favor

Prophetic Encounters

Additional copies of this book and other
book titles from DESTINY IMAGE are
available at your local bookstore.

Call toll-free: 1-800-722-6774.

Send a request for a catalog to:

Destiny Image® Publishers, Inc.

P.O. Box 310
Shippensburg, PA 17257-0310

*"Speaking to the Purposes of God for This
Generation and for the Generations to Come."*

For a complete list of our titles,
visit us at www.destinyimage.com.